Gladys L. Lahee

Birthday and Christmas, 1918

2445

# HISTORY OF THE WORLD WAR

### THE DECISIVE FACTOR?

Admiral Von Tirpitz long clung to the belief that the German submarine would be the decisive factor in the war, but was reported to have abandoned this opinion toward the close of the year 1917. In many quarters there is growing conviction that the war will be decided in the air.

# HISTORY OF THE WORLD WAR

BY
## FRANK H. SIMONDS
AUTHOR OF "THEY SHALL NOT PASS"—VERDUN

*FULLY ILLUSTRATED*

## VOLUME TWO
## THE MAKING OF MIDDLE EUROPE

·GARDEN CITY          NEW YORK
DOUBLEDAY, PAGE & COMPANY
1918

# CONTENTS

## PART I

## CHAPTER I

### THE NEW PHASE

## CHAPTER II

### THE TRANSFORMATION

## CHAPTER III

### NAVAL HISTORY

## CHAPTER IV

### SEA POWER AND THE GERMAN PLACE IN THE SUN

## CHAPTER V

### SUBMARINES

I. THE GERMAN CASE. German desperation at end of 1914—British sea power will throttle Germany—Germany's two submarine policies and what each promised. II. GERMAN POLICY. Germany commandeers her wheat—Britain declares wheat contraband—Germany retaliates by submarine and mine blockade of Britain—Both sides violate international law—International law knows not submarine warfare—Neutrals at first are forbearing and impartial. III. "RUTHLESSNESS." Extension of submarine campaign "necessary" in German eyes—They miscalculate degree of neutral complaisance—*Lusitania* Massacre arouses America. IV. AMERICA AND GERMANY. The American attitude at first uncertain—*Lusitania* incident definitely alienates America—Influence of Tirpitz waxes, then wanes, then becomes all-powerful, to Germany's cost . . . . . . .

## CHAPTER VI

### THE BATTLE OF THE DUNAJEC

I. THE EASTERN SITUATION. The importance of Dunajec. II. GERMAN TACTICS. Mackensen learns from French—Massed artillery bombardment—A mobile battering ram—Mackensen's "Phalanx" —The resistless German centre. III. THE GREAT BLOW. The three Russian armies—Dimitrieff's position—His annihilation. IV. BRUSILOFF ESCAPES. Germans cross the Wislok, then the Wistok —Reserves from Przemysl save Brusiloff—The Battle of the San— Russians evacuate Przemysl. V. LEMBERG. Russia's 1914 tactics reversed by Mackensen—Germany frees Galicia—Austria is saved— As Tannenberg saved Prussia, so Dunajec saves Austria . . . .

## CHAPTER VII

### ITALY DECIDES

I. 1813-1915. Italy declares war on Austria—Italy's interests and sympathies—The popular decision a wise one. II. YOUNG ITALY. Her people ill-satisfied with her political position—National ambition to redeem Trent, Trieste, Dalmatia—The ancient enemy in Vienna is encouraged in Berlin. III. ITALY AND THE TRIPLE ALLIANCE. A marriage of convenience—Her allies oppose—Italy's Libyan War—

# CONTENTS

## CHAPTER VIII

### GALLIPOLI

## CHAPTER IX

### RUSSIAN COLLAPSE

## CHAPTER X

### THE BATTLES OF YPRES

## CHAPTER XI

### THE WESTERN OFFENSIVE

## CHAPTER XII

### BACK TO THE BALKANS

## CHAPTER XIII

### THE SERBIAN TRAGEDY

## CHAPTER XIV

### THE END OF THE CAMPAIGN

# LIST OF MAPS

# LIST OF ILLUSTRATIONS

## LIST OF ILLUSTRATIONS

# PART ONE
# HISTORY OF THE WORLD WAR
BY
FRANK H. SIMONDS

# CHAPTER ONE

## THE NEW PHASE

### I

### RETROSPECT AND PROSPECT

From August, 1914, to the closing days of April, 1915, the history of the World War is the history of the German attack upon France and of the consequence of the failure of this attack in that great battle of arrest, the struggle at the Marne. The gigantic conflicts in France, in Belgium, the struggles in Poland, East Prussia, Galicia, these were but logical consequences of the decision of the German General Staff to stake all, risk all, win or lose all, on the narrow front between the Straits of Dover and the Swiss frontier.

When the German General Staff made this decision, sweeping away all moral and political considerations involved in the violation of Belgian neutrality, there was a clear perception by them that if they failed, a thing unthinkable of itself, it was conceivable that Russia would destroy Austrian military power and in addition invade East Prussia. Six weeks of immunity from attacks in the east, six weeks in which Paris might be taken and the French military establishment destroyed, this was the calculation of the German military power, a calculation that at moments seemed almost realized, but in the end escaped all realization, when Kluck turned back from Paris for Soissons.

Thenceforth the war became a confused and involved series of battles, great in themselves but indecisive in their character, and inexplicable to a world public still seeking a Sedan or a Waterloo and far from realizing that Europe was just on the threshold of one of the long complicated wars, in which exhaustion rather than military decision might in the end terminate the fighting.

Actually, what occurred in these months is unmistakable. The failure of Russia at Tannenberg permitted the Germans to ignore the eastern

3

battle ground for many months, the lack of men and munitions on the part of the French and of the British enabled the Germans to seek from October to December to reopen the decision of the Marne. But in the end the complete breakdown of Austrian military power under Russian assault necessitated the transfer of German activity to the east and Germany accepted a defensive war on the west, while she sought, first to reorganize Austrian armies and then to dispose of Russia as decisively as she had sought to dispose of France in the Marne campaign.

This is the story of the eastern campaign from December, 1914, to the autumn of the following year, from the Battle of the Dunajec to the escape of the Russians about Vilna. Germany endeavoured to eliminate Russia as she had tried to dispose of France. Austria's necessities compelled her to go east while there was still hope, even real possibility, of a decision in the west. The slender force that held the Allied line in Flanders was all but blotted out when Germany at last gave over her assaults at the Yser and about Ypres. The British army had not been broken, but it had been well-nigh annihilated. And many months were to pass before the first considerable contributions of the new British armies were to be made to Field Marshal French's skeleton battalions.

But perforce Germany was condemned to the defensive on the west and in Artois in May and June, and again in Champagne and Artois in September, she had to endure great attacks, which all but opened a road through her trench lines and nearly brought to an end the deadlock in the west. Yet in the end her lines just held, her troops in the west by their tenacious and successful defensive enabled those in the east to win the most spectacular European victory since Sedan and to conquer more territory than had fallen to victorious European armies in any campaign since the days of the great Napoleon.

Nor was this all. A feeble and amateur venture into higher strategy on the part of the Allies at Gallipoli, the effort to prosecute an undertaking which could not succeed and was as much beyond Allied resources as a promenade to Berlin, drew German attention to the Balkans and prompted German and Austrian commanders to resolve on a campaign which was to open the corridor from Berlin to Stamboul and to

Bagdad, thus consolidating German power from the Baltic to the Persian Gulf.

Between May-day, 1915, and New Year's, 1916, German soldiers were to overturn the political situation of Central Europe and to modify the markings of the map as only the soldiers of the Revolution and the First Empire had modified them in the thousand years separating Otto the Great from William II. Actually, they were to transfer from the realm of hope and dream to the world of accomplished fact all the visions and aspirations of those German patriots, poets, and soldiers who had longed to see the restoration of the ancient German Empire of the remoter centuries.

## II. MIDDLE EUROPE

In this new phase which we are now to examine we are to see the creation of one more of those mighty empires which from Charlemagne to Napoleon have been constructed upon the soil of Old Europe. But this new empire was in one respect markedly different from all that had preceded since the days of Rome itself. It was not primarily built about or by one great man. William II was neither a Napoleon nor a Charlemagne. In certain respects, indeed, he did not differ from the least of his subjects—all were servants and workers in a system and in a machine which was itself the genesis of this new empire.

It is to Rome that one must turn for a parallel to this new German phenomenon which now filled Europe and carried its influence to the remotest corners of the world. Before the war, German influence in Constantinople had become supreme. When Russia turned from the Balkans to Asia in the last century, the British had ceased to concern themselves with the Sublime Porte; they had, quite unconsciously to be sure, evacuated Constantinople, and in their place the German came. The army of the Osmanli had been reorganized by the soldiers of the Kaiser. Far down in Asia Minor, by the famous Cilician Gates through which Alexander the Great had passed in his mighty invasion, German engineers had pushed the Bagdad Railway, which was first to enable German civil administrators to reorganize Turkey while German soldiers reconstituted the Turkish army, and eventually to permit a German-led attack upon Egypt from Syria and upon India by the Persian Gulf, along the road trod by the soldiers of Alexander.

All this was before the war.   When the war came, Turkey responded to German impulse and the Osmanli entered the conflict as the ally of the Teuton.   Even more impressive was the penetration of Austria-Hungary by the German influence. Austro-Hungarian military power had been broken at Lemberg; it had suffered defeats humiliating and complete at the hands of the Serbs on two fatal fields.   Reorganized in part by the Germans, Austrian and Hungarian armies had gone to new defeats which lost Galicia well-nigh completely and included the impressive capitulation of Przemysl, where an army almost as large as that of Napoleon III at Sedan, laid down its arms.

It was then that Germany was led, by force of circumstances but doubtless with a full recognition of the ultimate possibilities, to assume the mastery of the whole military establishment of Austria-Hungary. Austrian generals disappeared, even archdukes vanished or accepted honorific positions which only partially concealed their subservience to German generals.

Austrian armies were stiffened by German contingents, German divisions were introduced in Austrian armies, and the interpenetration extended to smaller units.   Here, in a restricted period of time, was a conquest more complete than had been expected in France or realized subsequently in Russia.   First his military establishment and then his political independence, so far as the making of war policies was concerned, passed out of the hands of the Austrian.   Vienna gave way to Berlin; Austrian diplomacy, like Austrian strategy, was made in Germany; and Austrian ambassadors the world over, and conspicuously in Washington, became only the agents and servants of German policy.

From this there was no escape.   Under the assault of Russia, Austria had almost collapsed.   Her Slav populations had disclosed a disloyalty which threatened extinction of Hapsburg imperial unity.   The attack of Italy, soon to come, was to open one more deadly peril.   Rumania, still neutral, continued to look over into Hungarian provinces with unmistakably growing appetite.   The Austrian German and the Hungarian

Magyar, the elements which had ruled although they were a minority in the Austrian Empire, could only preserve the semblance and shadow of their ancient power by the aid of the German, and it was inevitable that the German, called upon to make greater and greater contributions of men and of money to the Austrian, should demand the right to supervise the expenditure of both.

Thus, in the period between the Dunajec and Verdun, we are to see the conquest of Austria and of Hungary by the German; peaceful, logical, ineluctable; stirring heartburnings and jealousies in Vienna and apprehensions in Budapest, but, despite all this, meeting no real opposition since none was possible, for if the eventual extinction of Hapsburg independence was plainly forecast, yet to resist it was to invite Russian armies to the Hungarian plains, Italian hosts to the Istrian and Dalmatian littoral, and Rumanian divisions to the Transylvanian marches.

### III.  BERLIN TO BAGDAD

To the political and military assimilation of Austria-Hungary by pacific penetration there was soon added the similar absorption of Turkey and Bulgaria.  Turkey, assailed by Allied troops at the Dardanelles, and facing Russian invasion at the Armenian frontier, inevitably turned to Berlin for aid.  And when that aid came, when the slender Serbian barrier was demolished and the road from Berlin to Constantinople was open, it was natural that the liberator should, in turn, become the master, and Turkish policy, like Austrian, become, in fact, of German making.

Nor was the Bulgarian case different.  Ferdinand had made his bargain with the German.  He had his reward when German and Austrian troops joined his in Serbia and the Bulgarian people saw the odious Macedonian articles of the Treaty of Bucharest abolished.  Monastir, Uskub, Ochrida, received his garrisons.  Southern Serbia was joined to the Bulgar Czardom and, under German driving, even the obstinate Turk levelled the fortifications of Adrianople and ceded to Ferdinand that strip along the Maritza which gave Bulgaria a railroad to the Ægean on her own territory.

But in accepting this long-sought boon at German hands, Ferdinand had invited new and deadly perils.   He had made a foe of Russia; he had involved himself in war with Great Britain and with France; he had assumed responsibility for the destruction of Serbia and had thus made it inevitable that the Allies should henceforth make Serbia their soldier in the Balkans to the utter ignoring of all Bulgarian aspirations and interests.   Against the new powerful enemies Germany was the sole barrier and bulwark.   Actually Bulgaria had bartered her freedom against certain provinces and cities.   These she could hold only with the aid of their donor, and while she held them she was exposed to all the dangers incident to the hostilities of the nations fighting Germany—above all, to the hostility of Russia, always the nearest and the deadliest peril to the Bulgar State.  Thus, in gaining provinces, Bulgaria had lost independence. And, in the nature of things, the Bulgarian army, like the Turkish and the Austro-Hungarian, passed under German control; its strategy, its high command were no more its own; it marched and fought at the dictation of Berlin.

The fall of Serbia completed the creation of this vast empire which tardily but emphatically claimed the attention of the statesmen of the nations fighting Germany.   Uninterruptedly German will and German purpose ruled from Berlin to Bagdad.   On the western front the Germans erected against France and Britain a wall of trenches like to that which the Romans had in their later days stretched between the Danube and the Rhine to hold back the Germanic hordes.   Eastward, behind the marshes of the Pinsk and the Dwina, broken Russian armies held the field.   But these lines and the sea were the frontiers of the new central empire.

To Austria-Hungary, Bulgaria, Turkey—united to Germany voluntarily, through the pressure of their necessities or the urgings of their ambitions, at the outset—there was added, in the period we are now to examine, a vast area:   Russian Poland, Lithuania, a fraction of the Courland, and Volhynia, on the east; Serbia and Albania on the south. In addition, tragic Belgium was still under the German heel, as were most of the industrialized and mineralized districts of northern France.

At the apex of his power, Napoleon had never ruled over an empire comparable with this vast region which was now under the domination of the German. And at all times the Napoleonic edifice was founded upon the genius of the man who had made it. Those who most hated and feared Napoleon could, even in the midst of their sufferings and discomforts, confidently believe that the death of the Emperor would see the passing of his empire, as that of Alexander the Great had crumbled when the great Macedonian came to his inglorious end.

But this new empire was not even remotely connected with the personality of William II. It was the product of a system, not of a man; it was the product of a system that for more than a century had been growing in efficiency and in power, without regard to kings or generals. Kaiser, Field Marshal, Chancellor, all Germans were but the agents and servants of this centralizing spirit and this vitalizing efficiency. The soldier had not completed his victory before the functionary appeared to begin the organization of conquered ground and the absorption of this new district into the great central unity.

Such, in the large, was the great Middle Europe, which grew up, following the most marvelleous military successes since the Napoleonic era—which took shape in the period we are now to review.

## IV. THE GERMAN CONCEPTION

How much of this grandiose work was deliberate, how far this empire was constructed according to preconceived designs, how far it resulted from the accidents of military necessity, one may not say. Yet it is true that, long before the war, the German patriots had dreamed a new German Empire whose frontiers should, in fact, include the regions which were under German direction when the year 1915 closed.

One may look backward into the yellow files of Pan-German documents and find maps strangely prophetic of the Europe that is disclosed in the war maps of 1915 and 1916. Northern France and western Russia, Belgium and Russian Poland, together with Holland and Denmark, were included in the frontiers thus drawn, and the expansion of German influence through the Balkans to Anatolia and Mesopotamia was unmistakably foreshadowed.   A German place in the sun meant just this to the men whose policies and purposes had made the war inevitable.

But the fact is far more important than the dream which preceded. Whatever the dreamers of the past—whose visions were neither idle nor divorced from industrious effort, by Christmas, 1915, Germany had created this empire and by this date there had crystallized in Germany a determination to make the war map permanent.   Minor modifications of frontiers, retrocessions to France, more remotely conceivable an evacuation of Belgium, these were possible; but the essential integrity of this Middle Europe from the Meuse to the Beresina and the Niemen, from the Belt to the Persian Gulf, this was the fixed war aim of the German mind.

In this vast empire, with its millions of people, German order and German system were to prevail, and the achievement of Rome was to be repeated.   Slavs, Hungarians, Bulgars, Osmanli Turks, Arabs, all were to be organized in the German fashion; endowed with the real blessings born of German system, order, efficiency; the willing were to become partners, at least in a limited sense; the rebellious were to be crushed.   Such was the German conception, Augustan in its character, such was the fixed idea of thousands and hundreds of thousands, the idea of the leaders and makers of a Nation, not the personal ambition of a single individual.

This empire, comprising not less than 150,000,000 inhabitants, geographically compact, possessing within its boundaries enormous wealth in minerals, beyond the reach of sea power to threaten its internal communications, touching on the one hand the bleak north and on the other the deserts and tropics of Arabia and the once-flourishing region of Mesopotamia, pausing only temporarily at Suez and at the door of India, became, in the period between the Dunajec and Verdun, a solid fact.   It was the fact that the German perceived in all the time when the Allied press talked of his failures in Russia and its victories in France.   It was the grandiose reality beside which trench losses in Champagne and Russian escapes along the Dwina were insignificant.

When this empire had been completed, there was in the German mind but one more step necessary. Russia was for long months incapable of offensive campaigning, might in fact lapse to revolution or make a separate peace. Italy had been checked definitively. Britain was still unready. France only remained, and if there could be delivered against France one more blow, a blow as heavy as that which had been parried at the Marne, France might now fall, at the least might make a separate peace on terms which would not be too onerous. With France out, the safety and permanence of Mitteleuropa would be assured. Such was the spirit and reasoning of Germany when the period now under consideration came to an end. Such was the purpose in the German mind when she again turned westward to seek once more to reopen along the Meuse the decision of the Marne.

To understand this period nothing is more necessary than to dismiss those Allied notions which prevailed in that time—notions of a defeated Germany, conscious of its own impending ruin and already seized with madness and desperation. Nothing could be more false. Weary of the war the Germans were, but no more weary than the French people after Wagram and before Moscow. But victorious they certainly felt themselves to be, and the proof of their conclusion was for them written over the map of Europe in colours that were unmistakable. The Allies were taking trenches, the Germans were conquering provinces. The Allies were regaining hectares of lost France. The Germans were overrunning cities and districts so remote as to have only a vague meaning for the resident of Berlin or the peasant of Bavaria.

### V.  THE OTHER SIDE OF THE PICTURE

Another side of the picture there certainly was. In this period Germany failed to get an immediate decision in the east as she had failed at the Marne to dispose of France. A British army and a British nation were gathering strength each hour and each day, and this strength was to be exerted in unsuspected violence in a time that was to come. France was not broken in spirit and was stronger in reserves than the Germans suspected. Russia was to deal rude blows in a campaign further in the future than Germany could believe the war would extend.

Indeed, the very magnitude of the German success, coupled with the manner in which it had been won and the fashion in which German methods had aroused the hostile nations, had made it inevitable that the war should continue until there was an absolute German success, a conquest of Europe that deprived the conquered of all power of resistance, or a dissolution of this enormous empire and a restoration of the balance of power.   France perceived clearly that without this dissolution she would pass to the rank of a vassal of Germany.   Italy saw that her position would be exactly the same.   Britain recognized that her imperial edifice was doomed and her domestic security abolished if German power ruled on the Egyptian frontier and on the Belgian coast.

The magnitude of German victories in 1915, together with the brutality and violence of German methods in 1914 and 1915, at one time aroused the apprehensions and steeled the determination of her enemies. But in the summer and autumn of 1915 the Allies were still incapable of freeing France or saving Serbia.   They felt themselves victorious because they knew they were not beaten, but with the same spirit the German was able to look upon unmistakable conquests and undeniable victories.

We see then, in all this period, Allied weakness.   We shall see ineptitude and folly which made the German success possible.   We shall see a total inability to grasp the idea of Middle Europe which permitted British armies to be wasted at Gallipoli, when these armies might have saved Serbia at the Danube and prevented the opening of the road from Berlin to Bagdad.   Serbia was sacrificed, Bulgaria lost, Greece alienated by Allied blindness; the people of the Allied countries themselves were left in the dark as to the real nature of this new German Empire which was building, and, having long had their attention fixed upon trench lines and the most insignificant of local successes, woke suddenly to find a victorious Germany at Suez and in Bagdad, in Warsaw, Lemberg, and Belgrade, while despite their own desperate efforts, Lille, St. Quentin, and Laon contained Teutonic garrisons, and German shells still fell in Rheims, Soissons, Arras, and Ypres.

More than this; at the moment they perceived these things, the peoples of the Allied nations were to feel the weight of one more German offensive, more terrible than all that had preceded, and realize that, so far from approaching victory, they were still in danger of defeat.

Such briefly is the period which lies between the Battle of the Dunajec and the German attack upon Verdun; the period in which Germany—lacking a Napoleon in the field or a Bismarck in the cabinet, by virtue of the collective strength of its people, through the efficiency of its political system, and served always by the devotion of its sons— marched from conquest to conquest and from victory to victory until the German will was law alike in the capitals of Hohenzollern and Hapsburg, in the seats of power of the rulers of the ancient Caliphate and of the contemporary Osmanli Empire.

# CHAPTER TWO

## THE TRANSFORMATION

### I
### IN THE BEGINNING

The first months of the war were marked by such desperate fighting, by battles unequalled in the magnitude of the numbers engaged and the losses incurred—battles upon whose issue hung the fate of continents and the destiny of nations—that all mankind looked upon the amazing cycle of events, the early French defeats in Alsace-Lorraine, Belgium, and northern France; upon the Marne, the Aisne, and the Yser, with breathless attention, having little thought for the larger questions involved or the permanent meaning of this conflict in human history.

No one who lived through the days from the German attack upon Liége to the final defeat of the assault before Ypres, who read day by day the bulletins reporting battles greater than Austerlitz, Gettysburg, or Leipzig, can forget the tension and the strain of those hours, hours which, regard being had for modern means of communication, were probably the most interesting and the most crowded in all human history. Africa, Asia, the remote Pacific, and the little-known Indian Ocean furnished daily some new glory of heroism and some fresh horror of destruction.

From the moment when the army of Kluck emerged out of the cloud of official darkness, almost within sight of Paris, to the time when the Flanders struggle descended to a deadlock amidst fog and mud, the whole world viewed the German eruption as a super-Napoleonic drama. All the memories of the great struggles of a century before were translated into fact and familiar history repeated itself upon the pages of the daily newspaper.

But when at last winter and exhaustion had temporarily stayed the conflict, when artillery alone continued the battle from Switzerland to

the North Sea, and the contest was transferred to the remote Carpathians and to Poland, there came a transformation in the aspect of the
war to the minds of mankind generally.   It no longer seemed one more
of the struggles familiar in modern history—a struggle like those Europe
fought against Charles V, against Louis XIV, against Napoleon—a
struggle for the preservation of the balance of power and the prevention
of European supremacy by a single state or monarch.   Rather, it took on
the character of the remoter struggles of the Latin world against the bar-
barians coming down out of the North; of a struggle between savagery
—this time equipped with all the weapons of science—and unor-
ganized civilization.   First for the belligerents, directly assailed by Germany, then for the greater neutrals, and finally for more distant nations,
the war assumed the appearance of a struggle for existence—a struggle
against a common peril—until the roll of nations fighting Germany became a score, and, at the moment these lines are written, countries as
remote and little concerned with European rivalries as Siam and Liberia
have declared war against the German Empire.

## II.   BELGIUM

This transformation was due exclusively to the spirit disclosed by the
German people in making war and the methods employed by them in
prosecuting it; and the revelation of this spirit and this method had begun with the invasion of Belgium.

The invasion of Belgium had been a profound shock to the whole
world beyond the German frontiers.   The phrase of the Chancellor,
describing the German guarantee to observe the neutrality of Belgium
as a "scrap of paper," instantly gained and steadily held a place in the
memory of all the observers of a world conflagration.   It was naturally
coupled with his other assertion that the invasion was, in itself, a
wrong, but that Germany stood in the state of necessity, and German
necessity knew no law.

And had there been no subsequent horrors, no crimes against humanity and civilization; had the German armies conducted themselves in
Belgian territory with every regard for the rights and personal safety of

the Belgian people, the invasion of Belgium would still have stood as a reproach and a blot, because it was everywhere recognized as a violation of a national pledge and the invasion of a weak state by a powerful empire, not as an act of self-defence, but as a detail in a plan for the conquest of France.

With the invasion of Belgium a whole system of thought and of policy fell. To neutralize the weak nations, to give them the opportunity to preserve their independence and to live their own lives, withdrawn from the quarrels of the great, had been a part of Nineteenth-Century political morality. The maps of the ante-bellum period, solemnly shading Switzerland and Belgium in neutral gray as areas withdrawn from European strife, were not merely accepted as foundations of the new international doctrine, but as half-way marks on the road to a complete neutralizing of all states by the mutual accommodation of all old jealousies and the construction of a new confederation of the nations of the world. It was accepted as a beginning of the era of world peace by world consent.

When Germany invaded Belgium all this edifice went instantly to dust and ashes. Of a sudden the world stepped back into the Eighteenth Century, to the age of Napoleon, of Frederick the Great. Anew there was formulated the doctrine that force was the sole consideration, that small states had no rights when great nations were on the march, and that the lesser nationalities must again bow before the will of the strong nation armed.

In all neutral nations the invasion of Belgium deprived Germany of any moral advantage at the outset of the war. Her agents might protest, her champions argue, her statesmen explain; to all these explanations the world turned a deaf ear. The attack upon Belgium was perceived the world over to be an act of violence, not merely breaking down Belgian integrity, but also opening a breach in that wall which recent decades had sought to erect to prevent a relapse to the old, unhappy times of other centuries. There was a sense that, at a single bound, by reason of German policy, the world had leaped backward to the age of wars of conquest.

AFTER THE BATTLE OFF THE FALKLANDS

Von Spee's naval victory in November, 1914, off the coast of Chile, where the English Rear-Admiral Cradock and 1,500 men were lost, was amply avenged five weeks later off the Falkland Islands by Rear-Admiral Sturdee who sent to the bottom the *Scharnhorst*, *Gneisenau*, and *Leipzig* with 1,800 of their crews. This picture of the sinking *Scharnhorst* was taken from H. M. S. *Invincible*, whose boats may be seen picking up the German survivors.

## THE VOYAGE OF A TORPEDO—I

This torpedo left its tube on a British battleship only a fraction of a second ago. It is just taking the water, with propeller blades already rapidly whirling

## THE VOYAGE OF A TORPEDO—II

A white streak like the two shown in this picture strikes terror to the hearts of modern sea-farers. It is the tell-tale wake of a torpedo. In this case two have been fired from the United States battleship *Texas* while at target practice, and the picture has been taken from her deck. The white water is foam churned up by the rapidly revolving blades of the torpedo's propeller.

## THE VOYAGE OF A TORPEDO—III

A head-on view of a torpedo, taken from the target. Needless to say this one was fired for practice only and is unloaded, else camera and photographer would have been blown into a million fragments an instant after the click of the shutter. In target practice the unloaded torpedoes are picked up, for subsequent use, when their power is exhausted.

## BOMBARDING THE TURKISH BATTERIES AT THE DARDANELLES

This picture was taken in the spring of 1915 from the deck of the British dreadnought *Canopus* at the Dardanelles. A 12-inch gun has just been discharged in answer to the fire from the Turkish batteries. This ship has since been lost

THE ENGLISH BATTLE CRUISER *QUEEN MARY*

Lost in the Battle of Jutland, May 31, 1916, with about 1,000 men. Besides her equipment of 10-inch guns, she had eight 13½-inch guns and three torpedo tubes. Her armour-belt was 9 inches thick. Her displacement was 28,850 tons, her indicated horse-power 78,000, and her speed 28 knots.

*Copyright by American Press Association*

GUNS OF A BRITISH BATTLESHIP FROM THE FIGHTING TOP

This is the stern of the ship. Two turrets are seen, one elevated slightly above the other. There are two big guns in each. The turrets revolve so the guns may be aimed in almost any direction. The odd-looking circles strung on wires are part of the "wireless" equipment.

GERMAN BATTLESHIP FIRING A BROADSIDE AT TARGET PRACTICE

BRITISH BATTLESHIPS BOMBARDING THE GERMAN POSITION ON THE BELGIAN COAST

The land and naval forces were here able to coöperate to excellent effect in the early days of the war. "The first blow [in the Battle of Flanders] fell upon the seacoast south of Ostend. . . . A British fleet took station beyond the dunes and with its heavy artillery beat down the German advance after a slaughter which was terrible."

CHURCH ON THE *QUEEN ELIZABETH* IN THE DARDANELLES

The muzzles of two 15-inch guns jut out through the midst of the congregation. "*Big Lizzie*" or "*Black Bess*," as she is called by the sailors, did excellent service during the ill-fated attempt to force a passage through the Dardanelles (February and March, 1915). She fired her shells from the open Ægean, over the hill, a distance of twelve miles, and dropped them nearly on Fort Kalid Bahr, at the entrance to the narrows.

## THE GRAND FLEET OF THE BRITISH NAVY GOES TO SEA

The ships go forward in double column, perfectly aligned, with the flagship, *Iron Duke*, leading. She is a super-dreadnought, and carries ten $13\frac{1}{2}$-inch guns, twelve 6-inch guns, and five torpedo tubes; her displacement is 25,000 tons; her maximum speed 21 knots; and her armour-belt is extraordinarily thick—$13\frac{1}{2}$ inches.
The *Iron Duke* was Admiral Sir John Jellicoe's flagship at the battle of Jutland, May 31, 1916.

## BIRD'S-EYE VIEW OF A MAN-OF-WAR'S DECK

Visitors' day on the light cruiser, *Melbourne*, of the Australian navy

BATTLESHIP FIRING A BROADSIDE

The shock of a modern broadside is terrific. At target practice it is part of the routine to prepare for heavy firing by removing pictures from the ward-room walls, screwing the ports tightly closed, etc. Even with these precautions, some glass is always broken. The men cram their ears with cotton to prevent the rupture of their ear-drums. Sometimes a gunner is thrown to the deck by the concussion. A story is told of a photographer who was one day lifted bodily, camera and all, and thrown into the sea, when a broadside was fired.

While there was no other question than that of abstract right, while men were still thrilled with the reports of Belgian resistance and not yet aware of what German soldiers were doing in the Belgian Kingdom, the judgment of the world ran on the German attack upon Belgium, and in the Americas, as elsewhere, public sentiment turned against Germany. This revulsion of feeling was to have a profound effect in the future. It was to prove the first in the long series of steps by which the American nation marched toward conflict with Germany, because it felt that Germany had become the common danger for all democratic nations and equally the enemy of all nations which served republican ideals.

It is not an exaggeration to say that the German General Staff, when it decided to ignore moral considerations and invade Belgium, insured the verdict of mankind against Germany—a verdict possibly of no immediate weight if Germany won the war, but a verdict bound to have material as well as spiritual consequences if the gamble turned out badly and the passage of Belgium were not followed by the arrival in Paris. Thus we must recognize in the invasion of Belgium the first and the most important in that long series of events which were to end by alienating from Germany the sympathy of nearly the whole civilized world and enlisting one after another of the nations against her, until the United States, one of the most remote and the least materially interested of all, should draw its sword and send an expeditionary army to fight the German hosts upon European soil.

### III. LOUVAIN

But the invasion of Belgium promptly became a minor episode. Soon the press of the world was filled with the stories of what German armies were doing in Belgium and northern France. Tales of cities burned, women and children murdered, women outraged, civilians executed; reports of the reign of terror wherever German armies penetrated, became the common property of all educated men and women the world over.

As a culmination to these horrors there came presently the tragic story of the massacre and burning at Louvain. Of itself, Louvain is interesting and significant only as a larger and more clearly perceived example of what took place in scores of French and Belgian villages, towns, and cities.

The origin of the Louvain crime remains obscure. Apparently German troops, returning from a fight with the Belgians to the north, were mistaken by other German troops for the enemy and fired upon. This firing was attributed to Belgian civilians and thereupon began a reprisal worthy of the best achievement in infamy of any age.

In the slaughter that followed either age nor sex nor condition was respected. Women were turned over to the soldiers to wreak their will as a matter of discipline, children were slain, old men and young massacred, while whole quarters of the town were consigned to flames.

What was now done in Louvain had already been done in many other Belgian communities. What was sought was not to be mistaken. Belgium had resisted, the Belgian soldiers had fought instead of dispersing when German armies had sought passage through their country. A revolt in Belgium, barely possible now that the mass of the German armies had passed on, might threaten the German cause. The remedy was found in resort to a system of terrorism, to that peculiarly German method which has been identified by all other races as "Ruthlessness."

Louvain was only a symbol. Actually the same spirit was disclosed in scores of places and upon many thousands of men and women. Although Louvain was long closed to the inquiring witnesses of neutral nations, the German retreat after the Marne permitted the investigation of other towns where the method had been employed. In Lorraine, in Champagne, wretched survivors and smoking ruins of Sermaize, of Gerbéviller, of a score of villages and towns, equally testified to German presence and German method.

When the German armies crossed the French frontiers they were preceded by hosts of fleeing Belgians, already crazed by the knowledge of what had taken place in towns the Germans had occupied. All during the Marne campaign the roads behind the battle lines were filled with the women and children, with old men and young, fleeing as the Latin world had fled before another barbarism which also had a Teutonic origin and similarly employed the system of ruthlessness.

Nor were brutality to helpless human beings and violence to women the sole characteristics; not only were towns burned to terrorize districts, to impress upon the French mind the power and the force of an unconquerable Germany; but where the invaders did not destroy they defiled. The homes of the poor, the bedrooms of the insignificant, quite as much as the châteaux of the rich and the residences of the prosperous, were made the depositories of filth; and the most high-placed officers found pleasure in committing offences against common decency which in children are cured by corporal punishment.

In all this there was only in minor part the evidence of that lack of restraint which belongs to soldiery and has made invasion, even in civilized warfare, a curse and a horror. The worst crimes committed were committed not by brutes escaping from discipline, but by soldiers obeying orders. They were not accidents of war, but details in a carefully compiled plan of making war. They expressed the conclusion of the German mind that the way to conquer a foe was to terrify him, that the way to rob his arm of strength and his spirit of determination was to burn, to rape, to rob, and to murder, until the spirit broke and the soldier laid down his arms to escape a continuation of horrors wreaked upon his women and children.

It was but another manifestation of the same spirit which prompted the Germans, when the Marne was lost and the retreat had come, to turn their artillery against the cathedral at Rheims and begin the systematic destruction of this glorious monument of an ancient world, a destruction which was to continue more than three years. To murder the weak, to dishonour the helpless, to destroy the beautiful; such, it seemed, were to the German mind necessary steps in conquering a foe in the field and destroying an army and a nation.

### IV. THE "LUSITANIA"

The reports of German "terribleness" in Belgium and France were not immediately accepted by the outside world. Even England long remained incredulous, and not until the Bryce Report set forth the full and duly-proven evidence did the British public accept the testimony of its Belgian and French Allies, confirmed by the reports of British soldiers in Belgium.

Even this testimony might have been rejected by neutral nations had not the invasion of Belgium undermined German credit in the world and the subsequent sinking of the *Lusitania* served to confirm in the minds of men all the worst that had been alleged against German soldiery in Belgium and France.   The narration of the *Lusitania* Massacre belongs to the discussion of America's relation to the war, but the moral effect must be emphasized in any discussion of the transformation of the war due to German methods.

This murder of some hundreds of women, children, and non-combatants, many of them citizens of neutral nations; their slaughter in the open sunlight of the whole world, was an offence that could neither be concealed nor explained.   The echo of German songs wherever Germans gathered, celebrating this *Lusitania* killing, served to demonstrate how wide was the gulf opening between German and non-German mankind.

When to this crime against the laws of humanity and of nations there was promptly added that of Ypres, where the Germans employed poison gas, forbidden by every convention of civilized warfare, the transformation of the war for the British people and for a great and growing fraction of the American public, was accomplished.   Zeppelin raids on London, the bombardment of unoffending and open sea resorts, ultimately the enslavement and deportation of the Belgian people into Germany, were but natural and logical extensions of the German method.   They merely gave new force to the argument that the war was a war of moral, not material, interests—a war for civilization and against barbarism.

Stripped of all else, the German spirit, as it revealed itself in these and other incidents, seemed to contemporary mankind unmistakably the assertion of the doctrine that all conventions of humanity, all pledges of national faith, all restrictions of international law, became null and void when they conflicted with a German policy or interfered with a German purpose.   Crimes which should have put the guilty beyond the pale of human society, became meritorious acts when performed by German soldiers and sailors in obedience to orders and in conformity with German plans. Deeds, inhuman beyond all palliation, took on an heroic aspect for the German public when they served to terrorize occupied districts, thereby releasing fighting men for the front. The murder of women and children, the violation of women, the destruction of the homes of the poor and the insignificant, the slaughter of neutral women and children at sea; all means and methods included in the German term of "ruthlessness" were justified, defended, exalted, when they served a German end, and at rare intervals when the offence itself passed the ample German powers of justification, imaginary offences were alleged, after the fact, to explain outrages which were indefensible even on the basis of the invented provocations.

The consequences of this German spirit and method were patent when the period we are now to examine opened. A host of German agents, spies, servants, the ablest of German diplomats and the most astute of German ministers, aided by German residents and fortified by every resource of corruption, were unable permanently to combat the opposition and the hostility aroused in neutral nations. The German policy compelled neutral governments to act in defence of the lives and property of their citizens. The agents of the German Government attacked these governments, seeking to destroy them at home and with their own people. And in the end the governments were driven into open war with Germany, alike to preserve unity at home and to defend the lives and rights of their citizens abroad.

A monstrous German propaganda was conducted in Italy and the United States. Politicians were bought, all the resources of German commerce and finance were invoked, but again and again German intrigue abroad was confounded by German action in Europe. Italy entered the war on the very morning of the *Lusitania*, the German case was destroyed in America by this and succeeding crimes which steadily brought America to a realization of the actual character of the war and an acceptation of the European view.

In Europe the German methods nerved the French people to a

heroism and endurance unsuspected even of this brilliant people. Zeppelin raids, submarine slaughter, the poison gas of Ypres, wakened a sluggish Britain, first to unexpected response to the call for voluntary enlistment and then to conscription itself. Canadian survivors of the "gas attack" brought to America new and veracious reports of German methods, which found slow but sure credence as the meaning of the *Lusitania* Massacre came to the people of the United States.

### V. THE CONSEQUENCES

The consequences of the transformation of the war were not early perceived or justly appraised. It was not until Germany—victorious in the contemporary situation but palpably war weary—made the first peace gesture in the winter of 1916, that it became apparent how completely the war differed from preceding conflicts and how utterly Germany had become, for the peoples at war with her, an outlaw nation with whom it was impossible to negotiate in accordance with time-honoured usage, because peace by negotiation would permit Germany to escape from the consequences of her evil deeds and even, conceivably, to profit by methods which had roused the indignation and abhorrence of all civilized beings.

As the war progressed and more nations were drawn into the whirlpool, agreements were made between Germany's foes to right old wrongs, liberate subject peoples, remake the map of Europe. Utopian schemes were proposed, and schemes which were selfish. But when the Russian Revolution and the consequent restatement of Russian aims destroyed many of these arrangements, there still endured the determination to fight onward until this German purpose was obliterated, this German method discredited in the eyes of the German people, and either a German renunciation of "terribleness" or a German military defeat should put a term to a common peril of all civilized peoples.

To analyze the German spirit, to explain the use of these methods by a people which, before the war, had seemed substantially at one with all other civilized nations in respect of humanity and international faith, must be the work of the psychologist and historian of the future. Certainly it is beyond contemporary power, as it is outside of the resources of the present writer who has stood amidst the ruins of Gerbéviller and Sermaize and heard from eyewitnesses and participants the shameful story of German deeds in Belgium and France.

And yet despite the passions of the present hour one must perceive elements of grandeur amidst all that is repugnant and hateful in the German idea. The German people as a whole seemed to the world to have been seized with a vision of a magnified and glorified Germany— an ideal Germany for which they gave their blood and treasure without stint and without hesitation. Something of the spirit of the successors of Mohammed certainly shone through the achievements of German soldiers and teachers, who went forth to conquer, sword and torch in hand. They sacrificed life, liberty, the pursuit of happiness. They gave up all to serve that ideal German State, and they performed great deeds and mean deeds with equal self-abnegation. And however terrible in detail was this German conception, however regardless of the lives and the rights of other races, however contemptuous of the conventions of other generations, it still acquired a measure of dignity through the devotion it inspired.

Yet since this German ideal actually aimed at German supremacy in the world, the possession of Central Europe, the control of the land routes to Asia and Africa; since it assailed the existence of Frenchman, Belgian, Russian, Serbian; since it aimed at the ultimate destruction of the British Empire and the extinction of Italian aspirations; since, in the pursuit of German ends, it assailed the lives and property of neutrals and denied their right to sail the seas; since it employed methods, abhorrent to all mankind, to obtain ends dangerous to most nations, the whole world gradually took alarm and, one by one, nations far removed from the scene of actual conflict, and little concerned with European questions, took up arms against Germany.

All through the period which we are now to examine this process goes forward. All through this period German methods make new enemies, and the German people, on the morning of great victories, are faced with great combinations of nations, and hand in hand with this goes the ever-constant widening of the gulf between the German people and the rest

of mankind, between the German and the non-Teutonic mind.    Actually
the transformation of the character of the war was accomplished for
Europe by the spring of 1915.    The invasion of Belgium, Louvain, the
devastation of northern France, Rheims, the *Lusitania* Massacre, the
"poison gas" attack of Ypres; these are the stages.    By May, 1915, the
transformation is complete and the consequences still endure at the
opening of the fourth year of the World War, which sees the United
States among Germany's foes.

And even if it were conceivable that history should hereafter destroy
the contemporary judgments and Germany find justification for all
her deeds in the eyes of the future, this would not change the fact that the
transformation of the character of the war for the nations fighting in 1915,
and for those nations which were to enter it in 1916 and 1917, was one of
the dominating and controlling influences in the first three years of the
contest.    It was with the memory of Louvain, Rheims, and of the newly
lost provinces in mind that the French people fought on to and through
Verdun; it was with the *Lusitania* in mind and the Zeppelin raids in their
eyes that the British people created their volunteer armies; it was with
Belgium and the *Lusitania* in their thoughts that the United States first
endured the British interference with its commerce and remained the
magazine of the enemies of Germany and, at a later date, broke with its
oldest tradition and entered a European war.

# CHAPTER THREE

## NAVAL HISTORY

### I
### THE TEACHINGS OF THE PAST

Long before the outbreak of the World War Admiral Mahan had laid down the value of sea power in the wars of the past and estimated its prospective influence in the next war. For Britain and for Germany Admiral Mahan's volumes had become the law and the gospel in naval history, and to the first volume of this American sailor is ascribed the change of policy of the German Emperor, the decision to seek Germany's future on the sea, which led inexorably to the conflict between Teuton and Briton.

Sea power, in all the great conflicts of the past, had not been immediately decisive. Admiral Mahan had pointed out at great length and with a wealth of detail how the French were able, both under Louis XIV and Napoleon, to win, not alone campaigns, but temporary Continental supremacy, only to lose it in the end because they were unable to come to grips with sea power and, thereafter, on British soil, to crush their one implacable enemy.

In our own War of Independence the conclusive victory of Yorktown came when Britain had temporarily lost control of the waters of the American seaboard. Yet, by contrast, absolute supremacy at sea in 1870 did not avail to save the French because the decision on land was immediate and complete. In our own Civil War the North used its sea supremacy to the uttermost and the isolation of the South by blockade was the most potent single factor in the ultimate collapse of the Southern Confederacy.

And with the British declaration of war, in August, 1914, Germany became an isolated nation, so far as sea communication was concerned. First, her merchant marine was swept from the sea. Neutral harbours became the haven of the great liners which had carried German commerce and German prestige to the ends of the earth. The German flag disappeared from the ocean and the great ports of Hamburg and Bremen became as deserted as Charleston or Savannah in the Civil War epoch. All the vast trade in raw materials and in manufactured articles, the enormous export and import trade, which were the foundation of the prosperity of the new Germany and which had been created by the generation following the Franco-Prussian War, were paralyzed almost in an hour and remained paralyzed in the years of war that followed.

Next, within a time that was relatively brief, such German squadrons and cruisers as were at sea when the storm broke were methodically "mopped up." The *Emden*, the *Königsberg*, the *Karlsruhe* won fleeing fame and rivalled in destruction the exploits of the *Alabama*, but they were in turn remorselessly hunted down and destroyed, in the Indian Ocean, in the Rufigi River on the African coast, and in the South Atlantic. Admiral von Spee's squadron, escaping from a Japanese fleet and sweeping across the Southern Pacific, won a momentary success at Coronel, only to perish gloriously at Falkland Islands, in a fight that did honour to German seamanship and valour but revealed the hopeless inferiority of German naval strength. When this process of sweeping the seas was completed the oceans lay open to Allied commerce and were closed to German vessels of war and of commerce alike.

Never had a victory been more complete than that of the British navy in this first phase of the war, at sea. The old apprehension of a German raid upon British coasts, the idle but familiar legend of a contemplated German invasion of Britain, was revealed in its full absurdity. The accident of the mobilization of the whole British fleet at the moment of the outbreak of the war for its annual manœuvres; the rare good judgment of Winston Churchill, First Lord of the Admiralty, in countermanding the orders for demobilization and retaining the fleet in being during the critical days from July 25 to August 4, gave Britain, on the water, precisely that advantage Germany enjoyed on land, and abolished not merely the remote chance of a German attack upon Britain, but the very real danger that German cruisers might escape from their naval ports to the high seas and carry on a long and costly war upon British and Allied commerce.

In this phase of the war the British fleets accomplished what had been impossible a century before.   Villeneuve's fleet had eluded Nelson on a famous occasion, Napoleon had taken an army to Egypt and himself escaped to France at a critical moment in European history.   But under the new conditions of steam navigation the command of the sea by the supreme naval power had attained a degree of the absolute, unknown in history.   And so far as German commerce and German sea power were concerned this power was to remain absolute, even when the submarine began to take its toll of belligerent and neutral merchant marine.

## II.  THE CONSEQUENCES

The first consequence of this assertion of sea power was the successful despatch of the British army to France.   While the Grand Fleet moved majestically out of the vision of the world and took its station in northern Scotland, there to keep watch and ward, to take and retain a silent but remorseless grip upon the throat of German commerce, the lighter craft assured the safe passage of the Channel by Field Marshal Sir John French's army, transported with a speed and a success which established new records in this department of war.   From the outbreak of war to the end of the First Battle of Ypres not much less than 200,000 troops were thus ferried across the Channel, and their presence in France was essential to the safety of the whole Allied cause. Had these troops not arrived, France would have fallen.   At the moment when the western battle was reaching a crisis, the arrival of an Indian Army Corps brought from the Far East saved the day.   Thus, in a very real sense, the war on land was made possible for the Allies, and defeat was avoided, not merely by the valour of the troops at the front, but equally by the service of the British fleet.

Later the tide of Colonial support was in turn brought to Europe. Asia, Africa, Australia, Canada were able, as they had been always willing, to take their place beside the Mother Country on the French and Belgian fronts and elsewhere, when the flood of war turned to the Near East. In the first three years of the war not less than three million men were thus carried from all over the world to France and Belgium, and this mighty task was accomplished without the loss of a transport, while the passage from Boulogne to Folkestone, from Calais to Dover, continued as safe from German attack as the ferries in the North and East rivers of New York City.

Once more, as in the days of Louis XIV and Napoleon, Britain sat safe behind the silver ribbon of the Channel. Zeppelins and airplanes might at intervals reach her cities and exact their toll of lives, mainly of children and women; an occasional German raider might come down Channel or bombard a seacoast resort; but despite these hostile manifestations, Britain remained secure in her islands and gathered up her millions to strike her great foe.

Nor was the second consequence of supremacy at sea less important to the Allied cause. Germany had struck at her own hour and after full preparation. Her first blow had given her possession of the industrial districts of Belgium and northern France, the iron mines of Lorraine, the coal regions of Mons and Lens. She had in her grip the factories of Liége, of Lille, of Tourcoing, and of Roubaix. St. Quentin, all the great manufacturing districts of the valleys of the Scarpe, the Deule, the Scheldt, and the Sambre were at her disposal.

Thanks to the British fleet, however, this enormous initial advantage was promptly counterbalanced by the transformation of industrial America into the workshop, the arsenal, the granary of the Allies. In a few short months all the vast machinery of the great plants of the Western Republic were working for the Allies. Ammunition, guns, all the necessary implements and munitions of war were manufactured and transported across the ocean, until the whole western front met German attack with American rifles, American ammunition. The vast new armies of Britain were equipped in considerable part by America, and, thanks to this, were able to take their place upon the western front months in advance of the hour that they could have arrived save for American factories. What the British factories had done for the North in the Civil War, those of the United States did for Britain and France in the new world struggle.

Nor was the food supply less important. When the mobilization of an ever-growing percentage of the manhood of the warring nations brought with it diminishing food supplies, the United States, with Canada and Australia, supplied the Allied deficit. Thanks to the British fleet and the American wheat fields, the French people could still procure white bread long months after it had disappeared in Germany, and procure it at the ante-bellum price. When want invaded Germany, and privation, if not starvation, arrived; when the sufferings of the masses due to the blockade were very great, Britain still was well fed, and France had not yet begun to feel that need of economy in food which came only with the third winter of the war.

### III. THE NAPOLEONIC PRECEDENT

Because of this situation; because the sea power of Britain enabled America to feed and arm the Allies and thus deprive Germany of most of the advantage due to superior preparation and early military successes; because the people of Britain and France escaped hunger, while it already threatened the German people; because sea power, in fact, made all neutral nations the allies of the enemies of Germany, the sources of the arms and munitions employed to destroy German armies, Germany was in the end led to imitate the Napoleonic policy, which led to the downfall of the First Empire.

At Jena, Austerlitz, Wagram, Friedland, Napoleon won victories which brought Prussia, Austria, Russia, the Continent to his feet. But ever and again British money and British influence roused a new coalition and compelled a new war. And it was the effort to get at Britain which led him to Egypt, to Warsaw, at last to Moscow. It was his effort to compel the nations of the Continent to join France in closing their ports to British ships and British commerce, thus to destroy commercial Britain, that was his undoing.

We are accustomed to think that it was the insatiable ambition of Napoleon which led him to seize Hamburg and Danzig, to establish

French rule along the Adriatic, and deprive Austria of her Illyrian coast. But the purpose of the great Emperor was rather to lay hands upon all the doors by which British goods reached continental ports.    His Berlin and Milan decrees were provoked by British hostility and in these lay the seeds of his downfall.    To get at Britain, he had to deprive the German and Austrian States of their sea front; it was because of Russian refusal to accept the Napoleonic policy that the Moscow campaign was provoked.    The long and deadly wastage of the war in Spain was alike the consequence of a desire to close Spain and Portugal to British ships, and of the ability of the British themselves to transport armies to the Iberian peninsula.

Seeking to isolate Britain, Napoleon was led from campaign to campaign, from annexation to annexation.    He was brought to the necessity of destroying the commercial life, not merely or primarily of France, but of Russia, of Prussia, and of Austria; and, as a consequence, Austria, Russia, and Prussia were driven inexorably into alliance with Britain.    And ultimately, such an alliance, at Leipzig and Waterloo, destroyed Napoleon.

In precisely the same fashion the German situation led to a similar policy.    The neutral nations had become the arsenal and the granary of the Allies.    It was impossible for Germany, acting in accordance with international law, to prevent this.    It was the unquestioned right of neutral nations to trade with belligerents—it was not their fault that the British fleet had closed German ports.    No law, no conception of international law, warranted Germany in asking them to declare an embargo upon munitions, to abandon the policy Germany had pursued as recently as during the South African War.

And Germany could not blockade Britain.    Her sole weapon was the submarine; but to employ the submarine necessitated the sinking of neutral as well as belligerent ships, whether carrying contraband or merely engaged in lawful trade allowed by all the rules of civilized warfare.    German necessity, which had led German armies into Belgium to strike at France and thus insured British entrance into the war, now confronted a new obstacle, which carried with it an even deadlier peril, since it involved the ultimate defeat of Germany, so her statesmen and soldiers reasoned, if Britain in security could arm her millions and feed her population with American meat and wheat.

Thus we shall see Germany, in this present period, led, through the direct influence of British sea power, to one deed after another, to one policy after another, designed to interrupt the flow of munitions and food to Britain, provoked by the shadow of hunger at home while her great enemies still had plenty, but calculated to rouse the neutral nations of the earth, and destined, in the end, to bring the United States and a whole powerful group of other neutrals into the war on the Allied side and thus transform neutrals into enemies. By adopting a course designed to deprive Britain and France of the benefits flowing from intercourse with these neutrals, Germany, in the end, made war with neutrals inevitable.

This was the achievement of British sea power. It was, ultimately, a decisive influence in the progress of the war. It did produce conditions which led Germany to attack neutrals; it did bring other nations into the war as the German invasion of Belgium had mobilized British sentiment for war. But it was not until a later phase that the real importance of this consequence became clear to the world.

Yet, at the outset, it is essential to see the German conception. Only by a rapid dash through Belgium could Germany hope to win her war as she meant to win it. Since this was the plain fact, Germany disregarded her pledge, ignored the rights and liberties of Belgium, and made her progress from Liége to Mons and thence to the very gates of Paris. Her necessity justified, to German minds, that wrong to Belgium which was incidental.

When the end of the first land campaign had failed to bring a German victory, and a long war was certain, German defeat became a possibility if the United States and the other neutrals were to remain the sources of Allied munitions and weapons. Germany might not starve, but she was sure to be outgunned, outmunitioned, outnumbered, if she failed to achieve a decision before British and French and Russian armies could be equipped from America, while British and French millions were fed from American food sources.

The sole alternative was a "ruthless" submarine war, which would destroy British merchant marine engaged in American commerce and so terrify neutral and particularly American shipping that it would refrain from entering British and French waters and bringing food and munitions to the enemy. And as in the case of Belgium, Germany made her decision. In the case of Belgium she risked British entrance into the war. In the case of the submarine she risked the entrance of the United States and of other states. Again the German people and the German rulers argued themselves into the belief that they would derive the profit without encountering the peril of such a course. Again they deceived themselves.

The submarine war upon commerce belongs to another chapter, but its genesis is in the successful assertion by the British of sea power in the first phase of the war. Inexorably this led William II into the fatal pathways of Napoleon I. Inevitably, as in the case of the French Emperor, William II found himself, on the morrow of great victories, compelled to deal with fresh coalitions of foes. Thus, though the British armies were long in arriving, though France had to bear two years of agony before the new British hosts could begin, British sea power exerted an influence quite as great as Mahan had forecast, and without this British aid the French and Russians would have succumbed almost at the start, and thereafter whenever it had been withdrawn. This was Britain's great contribution over two years and its value cannot be exaggerated.

### IV. NAVAL ENCOUNTERS

The outbreak of the war saw the British fleet take its post in Scotch waters, facing the German ports. For the first days and weeks the whole world awaited a Trafalgar or a Salamis at sea, as it watched for a Waterloo or a Sedan on land. But the German fleet was too inferior in strength to challenge the British armada, and the Grand Fleet under Jellicoe dominated the North Sea. Not until the still-remote day of Jutland was the German High Seas Fleet to venture forth within range of British first-line squadrons. German strategy was from the outset to disclose itself as a strategy of waiting, a strategy which had for its chief

# THE NAVIES AT GALLIPOLI

H. M. S. *QUEEN ELIZABETH*

H. M. S. *IRRESISTIBLE*

H. M. S. *OCEAN*

SOME BRITISH SHIPS AT THE DARDANELLES

The *Irresistible* and *Ocean* were sunk by Turkish mines on March 18, 1915, the day when an attempt was made to force a passage through the Dardanelles. The crew of the *Irresistible* escaped, but the *Ocean* went down so quickly that most of her people were drowned.

Of this trio the great super-dreadnought *Queen Elizabeth* alone lived to fight another day, because she was too valuable to be subjected to the risks run by the other ships.

THE LONG, HARD ROAD TO CONSTANTINOPLE

Drawn for the "Independent" by Arthur Elder

"Dardanelles" and "Gallipoli" are words that will always evoke memories painful to the Allies. For here the naval attack of February and March, 1915, failed utterly, and three battleships with 2,000 lives were lost in a few hours. The combined attack by land and sea, which came later, was equally futile and far more disastrous. "The Gallipoli venture, first and last, used up not less than a quarter of a million British troops and cost more than 100,000 casualties on the British side alone."

A great deal of ancient history has been made in this region. Here the Greeks fought the Trojans in prehistoric times; here the Spartans defeated the Athenians in the eventful battle of Aegospotamos in 405 B. C.; and here Xerxes crossed from Asia to conquer Europe in 480 B. C., and Alexander crossed from Europe to conquer Asia in 334 B. C.

FRENCH BATTLESHIPS AT THE DARDANELLES

When this photograph was taken these ships were bombarding the Dardanelles forts, firing over the hill which forms the background of the picture. A glance at the picture-map on the opposite page will show the station of the French ships in the Gulf of Xeros, from which they destroyed Bulair fort, overlooking the entrance to the Sea of Marmora.

FRENCH HYDROAEROPLANE AND WARSHIPS AT THE DARDANELLES

This hydroaeroplane has been sent out by one of the ships to observe the effect of the bombardment

ON BOARD A CRUISER AT THE DARDANELLES

French marines directing the fire of a light, rapid-fire gun against the Turkish batteries on the shore

THE BRITISH FLEET AT ANCHOR OFF KUM KALE

The observer stands near the Dardanelles' entrance where the Allies easily won a foothold. "With no great trouble the first barrier was destroyed and the mine-sweepers entered the straits and began the work of clearing the channel for the larger ships. This work continued from February 19, until March 18, 1915, when the road was clear for the great attack. On this day the whole fleet steamed up the straits toward the narrows. It was the belief of naval officers that the long protracted bombardments had silenced the Turkish forts. They were promptly undeceived."

GERMAN SHIP CAPTURED BY THE BRITISH IN THE DARDANELLES

When her capture became inevitable, the Turks managed to torpedo her. This gaping hole just above the water-line is the result

ON BOARD A TRANSPORT STEAMING UP THE DARDANELLES

The uniforms and faces of these soldiers and sailors betray their English origin. They are some of the "Anzacs," who
fought and died devotedly, but in vain on the terrible Gallipoli peninsula

## FRENCH TROOPS LANDING AT THE DARDANELLES

This landing-place is on the Asiatic side of the straits, just inside of Kum Kale, at the mouth of the little River Menderes, which was called the Scamander when the Siege of Troy took place upon its banks. A fleet of transports lies in the offing and the dim land beyond is Cape Elles, on the European side of the straits, where Fort Sidd El Bahr (captured by the Allies) was located.

## AN EXPLODING MINE

This picture was taken from on board a British destroyer in the Dardanelles, at the instant a Turkish mine exploded within a few feet. Photographers in the World War have had many hairbreadth escapes, but few have missed death more narrowly than he who took this picture.

aim to weaken the British by successful attacks upon individual ships until resulting attrition should restore the balance between the two fleets.

Such strategy was wise and inevitable. Behind the sand banks and narrow channels of German shores, covered by the fortress of Heligoland (which a pacific Britain, unmindful of the future, had surrendered to Germany for a price, now become ridiculous), preserving by the Kiel Canal the sure entrance into the Baltic and the consequent supremacy in that sea, the German fleet waited. Winston Churchill might later utter bold words about "digging the rats out," but the task was beyond the capacity of a modern fleet, threatened with all the perils of contemporary naval warfare.

Thus the naval warfare resolved itself into minor encounters and incidental losses—none of real importance, none calculated to change the balance between the two fleets—and thus enable the Germans to risk all in that long-toasted encounter "The Day," when German was to meet Briton on the high seas and German victory doom a modern Carthage. Powerless to prevent British armies from crossing the Channel and British cruisers from sweeping the seas clear of German merchantmen, the Kaiser's navy was compelled to confine itself to filling the North Sea with mines, attacking isolated ships with submarines, and risking minor encounters with smaller units.

In this time the French fleet, in strict conformity with arrangements made before the war, arrangements cited by Sir Edward Grey when he declared that Germany must not attempt to come through the Channel or attack France unless with the clear recognition that Britain would intervene, took over the task of maintaining Allied security in the Mediterranean and sealing the Austrian fleet up within the Adriatic, a task that the French were to perform until the hour when Italy should enter the war and Italian squadrons take over a portion of this difficult task.

Yet before the French could assume the whole burden, their fleets had necessarily to cover the transportation of French troops from Algeria, Tunis, and Morocco to the home ports. And in this time there occurred an event which was fraught with fatal consequences. The German cruisers, the *Goeben* and *Breslau*, caught in the western Mediterranean at the onset of hostilities, fled to Messina, after having bombarded Bona and Philippeville on the Algerian coast. Ordered to leave the Italian port, they sailed to what seemed certain death, since a British squadron was in their pathway.

Yet, as a result of circumstances that can hardly fail to be a permanent ground for censure of the British Fleet, these ships escaped, reached the Dardanelles, passed them, and came to anchor in the Golden Horn. Having permitted them to get away, the British admiral failed to follow them into Turkish waters, risking Turkish resistance. As a result the *Goeben* and the *Breslau* became a decisive influence in driving Turkey into conflict with the Allies. The ships, retaining their German crews, passed to the Turkish navy. Presently they appeared in the Black Sea and, by attacking Russian ships, provoked a Russian declaration of war. In this incident is seen the first in the long series of failures and blunders which were to cost the Allies so dearly in the Near East. And even at the end of three years the explanation of the escape of these ships remains hidden.

By contrast, the dash of British smaller craft into the Bight of Heligoland and the sinking of two German cruisers was a detail, although the brilliance of the exploit filled Britain with pride at the moment. But British rejoicing was brief. Less than a month afterward one German submarine accounted for three large British boats, the *Cressy*, *Aboukir*, and *La Hogue*, under conditions that were again a reproach to British naval generalship, while in following weeks other British ships of greater value were victims of this new weapon. The war had not proceeded for two months before the British as well as the rest of the world were aware that, given her inferiority in resources, Germany was to prove no mean antagonist on Britain's own element.

At the moment of the German advance in Flanders, when the 1914 phase of western operations reached its crisis and the Kaiser and his hosts came pounding down from Antwerp on the road to Calais, the British fleet intervened and saved the Belgian army by sweeping the invaders from the road along the sand dunes which led by Nieuport to Boulogne.

But by far the most interesting and considerable naval operations between the outbreak of the war and Gallipoli were the two battles in South American waters, one at Coronel on the Pacific Coast, the other at the Falkland Islands. In the former, an inferior squadron of British boats, the antiquated *Monmouth* and *Good Hope*, accompanied by the *Glasgow*, which had little fighting value, and deprived of the doubtful aid of the *Canopus*, encountered the squadron of Admiral von Spee, which included the *Scharnhorst* and the *Gneisenau*, two swift and powerful cruisers, as well as the *Nuremberg*, *Dresden*, and *Leipzig*. The fight was short and the end complete. Admiral Cradock went down with his flagship, the *Good Hope;* the *Monmouth* shared the same fate; the *Glasgow* escaped. Once more there had been a blunder—the size and strength of the German Pacific squadron had been known, and to send such old and inadequate vessels to meet it was to send ships and men to certain doom.

The defeat was quickly avenged. Two new battle cruisers, the *Invincible* and *Inflexible*, were sent swiftly and secretly from England. With them went three armoured cruisers, the *Carnarvon*, *Kent*, and *Cornwall;* at sea this squadron, commanded by Admiral Sturdee, met the *Bristol* and then the *Glasgow*, the sole survivor of Cradock's battle. This considerable squadron entered the port of the Falkland Islands to coal and on the next day the squadron of Spee, seeking the *Canopus* and the *Glasgow*, appeared. Cradock had perished on November 1; on December 7 Spee's whole squadron, save for the *Dresden* which escaped and kept afloat until March, went down in a running fight. A few survivors were picked up by the victors, but most of the officers and men under Spee met a sailor's death after a brave but hopeless fight, quite as unequal as had been the struggle at Coronel. Thus an unnecessary defeat was avenged by a brilliant victory, and Germany's only squadron outside of home waters annihilated.

### V.   THE DARDANELLES

A single other naval venture alone commands attention in the first year and a half of war. The entrance of the *Goeben* and the *Breslau* into the Dardanelles had determined the decision of the Turks and the

Turkish declaration of war had isolated Russia. Germany, holding the mastery of the Baltic, her Osmanli ally master of the Bosporus and the Dardanelles, there was left to Russia only the remote ports of Archangel on the north and Vladivostok in the Far East. And both were closed for long periods by winter and neither could serve as the base for Russian armies.

Already, before the end of the autumn of 1914, Russia was beginning to feel the pinch for munitions and, since it was necessary to finance Russia in part, nothing was more essential than that Russian wheat should flow outward to balance the Allied credits and repay the Allied loans. Nor was it less necessary that the crushing of Turkey should be prompt, that Allied ascendancy in the Balkans might be maintained and Bulgarian stirring checked.

Were it possible then to force the Dardanelles, to push through with a fleet, as Admiral Duckworth had done a century before; to arrive before Constantinople, as a British fleet had done in the critical days of the last Russo-Turkish war when Russian armies were approaching the Golden Horn, the profit would warrant paying any reasonable price alike in ships and lives. Here, very concisely, were the terms of that great gamble, which was the naval attack upon the Dardanelles. It failed absolutely. One of its consequences, but not an inevitable consequence, was the subsequent land and sea attack, the ill-fated Gallipoli campaign, which brought such a train of evil and even of scandal.

Yet the original risk, accepted by Winston Churchill, whose imagination, as usual, passed his judgment, calling as it did for the risk of a few obsolete ships, supported by only one or two modern and first-line units, did not pass British and French resources; nor were the actual losses, as the event proved, sufficiently heavy to weaken in any measure either British or French sea establishment.

The real criticism of the Dardanelles affair is to be found, if at all, in the fact that all the lessons of naval warfare were against it. Sampson had declined a similar venture before Santiago when confronted by forts far inferior. Farragut had passed the forts at the mouth of the Mississippi, and New Orleans had fallen as a result; but in that earlier period, indeed down to the contemporary era, the menace of mines had been practically non-existent, and Farragut could without too great rashness say at Mobile: "Damn torpedoes, go ahead!" since the torpedo of the Civil War age was to be classed as well-nigh futile. But the Japanese at Port Arthur had not risked any forcing of the entrance.

More difficult than the entrance to Santiago or to Port Arthur, better defended as to forts and as to guns, since the defences had been the work of the German General Staff and German officers commanded many of the batteries of heavy guns, themselves the product of Krupp, the Dardanelles were in fact beyond the power of a fleet to reduce, and from the very outset the attempt was doomed to repulse. Since this was patent, plainly the wiser course would have been to wait until land forces were available and make a joint operation; and such a joint operation could have a chance of success only if it were not preceded by a naval attack without land aid, which would forewarn the Turks and lead to the immediate fortification of the Gallipoli peninsula and thus to the defeat of any land operations.

But in February, 1915, neither were land forces available nor was it easy to see whence they could be derived in any immediate future. When General Ian Hamilton's army was at last sent to the Gallipoli Peninsula it was not only inadequate for its task, but its departure weakened British armies in France, contributed to the failure of the British effort in Artois, and produced a situation in which Field Marshal Sir John French, on the evening of a day at Festubert, when he had lost thousands of men because his guns lacked ammunition to prepare an attack, received orders to send a considerable share of a non-existent reserve stock of shells to the Dardanelles.

And since men were lacking and the opportunity dazzled those who played with it, the fleet undertook an impossible task, failed, and gave it up, wisely and in time. Had there been no further venture, the Dardanelles experiment would have been a detail; indeed so unmistakably tremendous were the certain rewards of success that the judgment of those who ordered the attack might have been accepted. As it was, the

Dardanelles was the first step in one of the most gigantic blunders in military history and its consequences were fraught with incalculable harm to the Allies.

VI.   THE DEFEAT

The actual naval operation at the Dardanelles is simply told. About a hundred miles west of Constantinople the sea of Marmora narrows to a channel in places less than a mile wide and rarely more than three.   For sixty miles this channel winds to the Ægean, separating the Gallipoli Peninsula from the Asiatic mainland and at its mouth washing the shore, forever memorable as the scene of the Siege of Troy.   Through this channel the current runs southwestward at the rate of four miles an hour.   In the time of sailing ships this current was an obstacle to navigation, and it became a peril to the modern battleship when floating mines were adopted as an engine of destruction.

At the point where it enters the Ægean, this channel is several miles wide and it was imperfectly guarded by a few old forts, mounting guns of no real value against armoured ships.   But fourteen miles upstream the channel narrows to a pass hardly three quarters of a mile wide, and makes a sharp turn.   At this point, strongly reminiscent of the entrance to Santiago harbour, the Turks had erected a series of strong forts on either shore.   Here is the village of Nagara, on the site of the ancient Abydos; here Leander swam the straits to meet Hero; and here Lord Byron repeated the feat centuries later.   Here was the great obstacle— the sea gate to Constantinople.

Having assembled a fleet of French and British warships, mainly composed of ships mounting heavy guns but no longer in the first line, although there were also present the *Queen Elizabeth,* one of the newest British superdreadnoughts mounting fifteen-inch guns, and the *Inflexible,* which had shared in the winning of the Battle of Falkland Islands, the Allies, on February 19, began the work of silencing the forts at the entrance of the Straits, and the Plains of Troy and the hills that had looked down upon the Homeric struggle echoed to the roar of modern high explosives.

With no great trouble the first barrier was destroyed and the mine sweepers entered the Straits and began their work of clearing the channel for the larger ships. This work continued until March 18, when the road was clear for the great attack. On this day the whole fleet steamed up the Straits toward the narrows. It was the belief of the naval officers that the long-protracted bombardments had silenced the Turkish forts. They were promptly undeceived.

Suddenly all the forts opened fire. Soon three great shells fell upon the French ship *Bouvet* and at the same moment she touched one of the floating mines the Turks had launched. In three minutes the ship had disappeared, carrying most of her crew down with her. An hour later the *Irresistible* struck a mine; her crew escaped but the ship subsequently sank. Next the *Ocean* touched a mine, and she went down almost as quickly as the *Bouvet*. Meantime the French *Gaulois* and the British *Inflexible* had been put temporarily out of action by gunfire.

This was the end. Three battleships and two thousand lives had been lost and the Straits had not been forced; the forts had not been silenced; the peril of mines had not been surmounted. At the moment when the world was still looking for the arrival of the Allied fleet at the Golden Horn and the restoration of the Cross at St. Sofia on Easter Sunday, the Allied fleet had abandoned the task as impossible. Once more, as so often in his long European history, the "Sick Man of the East" had recovered on what had seemed his death bed.

This decisive defeat at the Dardanelles was the second in the series of Allied failures in the Near East; allowing the *Goeben* and the *Breslau* to escape had been the first. By this later failure, Allied prestige in the Balkans was dangerously impaired. In Sofia and Athens the defeat of sea power produced echoes which were not heard at the time, but were memorable at a later date.

Yet even after that failure, the dazzling lure remained. No man could exaggerate the value to the Allies of a victory that should open the sea gate of Constantinople and restore communication with Russia. Hence, when the fleet had failed, the temptation to try again, with an army to support the navy, was almost irresistible. It could not be resisted, because it had seized the mind and fired the imagination of one of the most brilliant, if most erratic, of Allied statesmen.  The first venture was to be ascribed to Winston Churchill, First Lord of the Admiralty.  He was now to push his project in the teeth of the opposition of Field Marshal Sir John French and General Joffre, and to draw away from the main front, at a critical hour, men and guns sadly needed in Artois.  But for the moment, while the new operation was preparing, the Gallipoli affair languished.

## CHAPTER FOUR

## SEA POWER, AND THE GERMAN PLACE IN THE SUN

I

### THE FAMILIAR STORY

In one other respect the dominant sea power in the present struggle repeated the familiar achievements of the past. In the long struggle between Britain and the House of Bourbon in the Eighteenth Century, France, frequently victorious in Europe and usually, although not always, fighting on enemy soil on the Continent, saw her overseas empire extinguished. India and Quebec were lost by the Old Monarchy, and Napoleon, having for a moment conquered Egypt and acquired Louisiana, was obliged to flee the former and sell the latter. Thanks to sea power Britain was able to wreck all the colonial aspirations and efforts of France at Plassey and on the Heights of Abraham, and at the end of the Napoleonic Wars France was once more restricted to the European Continent, after two centuries of colonial effort and no small temporary success.

The destruction of the German colonial edifice was much more prompt, as British control of the seas was more nearly absolute in the twentieth than in the preceding centuries. The very first week of the war saw the German colony of Togo in Anglo-French hands; thereafter in steady succession the other outlying possessions of the German Empire were conquered. With the outbreak of the war they were isolated from the Fatherland; thereafter it became merely a question of time until they should fall like ripe fruit into the hands of the enemy, and, though their defence was brave and the task of occupation arduous, by reason of distances, poor communications, and sparse population, there was never a moment of hope that German East Africa could escape the fate of Quebec, or the German Kamerun that of French India. From August, 1914, onward, the various colonies simply awaited the moment when the British and their allies should feel willing to spare the men and material for "Side Shows," for these minor campaigns necessary to extinguish German "places in the sun" of Africa and of Asia.

GERMANY'S FORMER POSSESSIONS IN THE PACIFIC

The black area shows Kaiser Wilhelm's Land and the other German possessions in the Pacific—now lost to her. Their proximity to Britain's "island-continent" explains why the Australians have resolved that this territory shall never be returned to Germany.

And there was one more notable detail in which these campaigns recalled the past. In her great struggles with France on the American Continent, Britain had been aided and even led on by her American colonists.

Now it was the Australians who crossed the narrow channels to seize the German islands to the northward.   New Zealand stretched a hand out to German Samoa; South Africa, having suppressed a German-incited rebellion, sent an army under Botha, the famous Boer commander now wearing the British uniform, to clean out German power and German intrigue from German Southwest Africa, as it later sent Smuts to repeat the achievement in German East Africa.

Aided in the Pacific by Japan and by her own Australasian subjects, in Africa by the Boer and British colonists alike, supported by French and Belgian troops in Central Africa, drawing upon East Indian and black troops, Britain slowly but surely dealt with the German overseas colonies.

And in all this there was nothing that rose to the level of a great campaign—there was nothing that suggested the glories of the Eighteenth Century struggles in India and America.   Nowhere had German occupation sent down the roots that French settlement had developed in America.   Brilliant achievements there were, achievements that gladden the sporting instinct of the Briton or delight those who love the romantic and picturesque.   Yet, in the main, the destruction of the German colonial empire was comparable with the absorption of a helpless victim by an anaconda.

It was the recognition of this very helplessness of their colonies that had made the Germans furious before the war; it was this helplessness beyond the seas which accentuated their passion when their victorious armies were approaching Warsaw and within reach of Constantinople, while their guns were still audible in Paris.

In all this, too, history did but repeat itself, and the German, familiar with his history, could feel even in victory something of the cold breath of the past which had blown in upon Napoleon's Empire and stayed the hand of the great conqueror.   Like Napoleon, William II could win battles and campaigns in Europe, but like Napoleon he was halted at the seashore, while beyond the range of his land guns he saw an empire disappear and, in addition to the empire which was German by possession, that other far more considerable empire which was the creation of the merchants, the bankers, and overseas representatives of that new commercial Germany, which on every sea and in every continent had been threatening British commerce. Small wonder was it that a German Hymn of Hate rose shrilly and even more shrilly as time went on.

## II. GERMANY'S PLACE IN THE SUN—MITTELAFRIKA

At the moment when the World War came, Germany had a far-flung circle of colonies. Murdered missionaries in China had been paid for by the cession of Kiaou-Chau, which was already raising its head as a rival to British possession and Japanese. A German Hong Kong in the making, a counterweight to Port Arthur newly won from Russia, Tsingtau was showing swift progress and extending a railway tentacle deep into Chinese territory. Southward, Germany had purchased from Spain the last remnant of her Pacific empire, the stray islands excluded by the United States from its purchases following the Spanish-American War. One of the Samoan group, the northeastern quarter of New Guinea, near Australia, these were the widely separated and comparatively insignificant colonial possessions of the Germans in the Far East, ridiculously insignificant to the German mind reflecting upon the European greatness of his country, when he contrasted them with British India, French Indo-China, American Philippines, Japanese Corea, or with the great English-speaking empire growing up to the south of Kaiser Wilhelm's Land.

But it was in Africa that the German had laid the foundations of a real empire, although even here his possessions seemed to him all too limited and scattered. A million square miles in area, Togo, Kamerun, German East Africa, and German Southwest Africa, were divided from each other, cut off from the fertile regions of the Congo Valley, walled in by British and French colonies vastly more desirable; or strangled by Portuguese and Belgian territories whose integrity was guaranteed by British and French treaties.

In the face of all this Germany had cherished a dream and conceived a plan. Already German patriots had constructed maps showing a German colony extending from the Indian Ocean to the Atlantic,

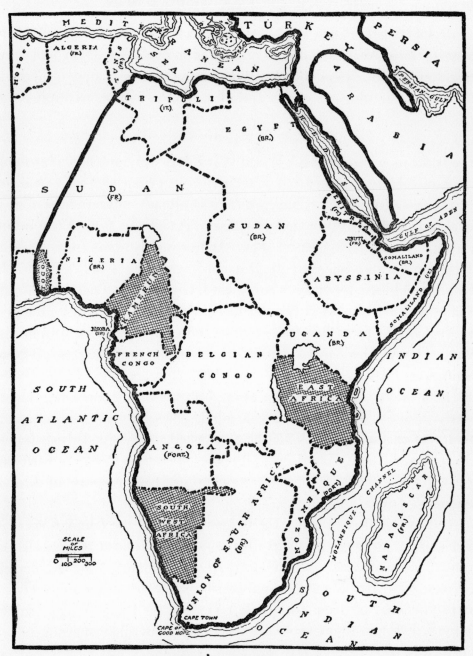

## GERMANY'S AFRICAN EMPIRE

The checkered areas show the German colonies at the outbreak of the war. In the first year of fighting the Germans were driven out of them all except East Africa in some parts of which they continued a stubborn resistance into the fourth year of the war.

The heavy black line incloses the African territory that Germany hoped to acquire. Note its junction with Turkey-in-Asia and thus with Middle Europe, through Egypt.

including Belgian Congo and French and British possessions between Stanley Falls and Lake Tchad.   Portuguese colonies on the east and west coasts were also marked with German colours.   Here, in the great basin of the Congo, including the headwaters of the Nile, extending from the Orange River to the mouth of the Niger on the west coast and from the Zambesi to the frontiers of Uganda on the east, the German had traced out a tentative place in the sun of Africa.

Nor did the dream end with this huge proposal.   In addition not a few German patriots, never reconciled to British conquest of the Transvaal and Orange Free State and firmly convinced that both states would welcome the chance to throw off British rule and exchange the yoke of King George for the sovereignty of the Kaiser, boldly coloured Africa with the German shade from the Cape of Good Hope to the borders of Egypt and spoke confidently of the time when this Mittelafrika would be joined to a Mitteleuropa, dominated by Germany, by way of the Bosporus and Suez, and Cecil Rhodes's dream have a German realization.

Meantime, Germany had already taken the first step toward the achievement of this colossal project.   In 1911, when the Agadir crisis had broken, Germany had, after vain efforts to claim a share of the Shereefian Empire, found her "compensation" for French Moroccan gains in the Congo and thrust forward two long tentacles across French territory, bringing German garrisons to the west banks of the Congo and Ubanghi rivers at the moment when a German railroad was approaching the eastern frontiers of the Belgian colony on Lake Tanganyika.   While Britain was intent upon realizing her Cape-to-Cairo project, Germany was preparing for the Transafrican railroad, which, unlike the long-contemplated French Transaharan condemned to desert regions, would tap some of the most fertile regions on the planet.

Behind all the commercial advantages lay the prospective hosts that Germany could enlist among the natives of the African empire under German officers, submitted to German training, equipped with all the resources of Krupp.   Already envious of the progress made by France in training Arab, Kabyle, and Negro troops, whose fighting qualities had been revealed in Europe in 1870, Germany contemplated organizing black armies which should sweep Africa from one end to the other and carry German power from Suez to Tangier, from Cairo to Cape Town.

If Germany, the Pan-Germans, nourished a dream of a restoration of the Old German Empire in Europe, of a Mitteleuropa which should stretch from the Channel to the eastern limits of Courland and Poland and from the Baltic to the Persian Gulf and Suez, the German Colonial Party had a vision of a Mittelafrika only less splendid, and there were not a few who dreamed that the two conceptions might be fused, when German armies, with Turkish aid, should enter Cairo and other German forces, armies created out of the boundless human reservoirs of Central Africa, should liberate the South African Republics, restore the Boers to the Teutonic world, and extinguish British power at the Cape.

### III.   THE FACT

Such was the vision.   But in July, 1914, the fact was still far different. In an African empire five times the area of the Fatherland the Germans had established less than 22,000 white settlers.   All the sea gates to these colonies were either held or watched by British possessions. Whalefish Bay, the one good harbour of German Southwest Africa, was British.   From Zanzibar the British dominated the coast of German East Africa, while the French in their Congo colony, the British in Nigeria, held the harbours of the west coast of Africa, from which railroads would eventually lead inland to the Congo basin.

In North Africa more than a million Europeans were settled under the French flag, and cities like Algiers, Oran, Tunis, calling places of German ships, contrasted unpleasantly for German pride with the little stations of German Africa.   Even Dakar, on the west coast, the coaling station for the South American trade, was French, while at Casablanca a new harbour and a new French base were rising.   At the other end of Africa another million of whites, British subjects, were opening a new empire which was moving northward toward the Congo valley with swift leaps along railroads which were already approaching the shore of Tanganyika.

Nor had his colonial rule, despite the construction of some rail-roads and a few model towns, been the success that the German had expected. The inability of the Teuton to deal with a subject race had produced one of the bloodiest of all wars between the white and the black in Africa. In German Southwest Africa the struggle with the Her-reros had ended only with the practical extermination of the native, and the colony had been left without labour when the terrible contest was over.

Yet it is but just to say that, before the outbreak of the war, there had been a growing realization in Germany that the African adventure had been badly conducted and that, unless new methods were employed, there could be no success comparable with that of France with its mil-lions of blacks in West Africa or with that of Britain all over the world. Tales of atrocities in their colonies had stirred the sluggish German pulse and men of the commercial rather than the military class were beginning to appear in colonial offices.

In the making of the colonial empire in Africa, Germany had already roused the fear of the Belgians, who saw their territory between the Atlantic and Lake Tanganyika the object of German design. Was it not Bernhardi who had suggested, long before the war, that merely by tak-ing the Congo Free State, Belgium had forfeited her right to have her territory in Europe respected? Portugal had shown alarm when the Germans had prevailed upon the British to agree to a partition of Portu-guese colonies when Portugal consented to sell them. Yet, the Germans later charged that Portuguese anxieties were stilled by a renewal of British promise to defend these colonies until Portugal wished to part with them.

France, after the Agadir affair, had seen her Congo territory muti-lated. Across that stretch of French territory which had hitherto ex-tended without interruption from Algiers to the shores of the Congo, the Germans had thrust two coils, and French Congo seemed, on the map and to the French mind, already enveloped in the folds of the German boa constrictor and doomed to ultimate disappearance. Already the Congo suggested to the French a second Quebec.

As for Britain, until the outbreak of the war she regarded the German

"HAVE MERCY, O DEVIL OF THE AIR!"

The World War has brought strange things to far corners of the earth. These natives of the French Congo are panic-stricken at their first glimpse of an aeroplane

DRIVING THE GERMANS FROM LAKE TANGANYIKA—I

Part of the British expedition on its way, crossing the reedy swamps of Lake Bangweolo, in northeastern Rhodesia. There were only twenty-seven white men in the party under Commander Simson, R. N., whose success earned him the D. S. O.

DRIVING THE GERMANS FROM LAKE TANGANYIKA—II

Bearers wading the shallows of Lake Bangweolo, with supplies for the expedition upon their heads. Livingstone died not far from here in 1873

A CONVOY IN THE EAST AFRICAN CAMPAIGN

Soon after this picture was taken this convoy was attacked by a German force, but successfully defended by British African and East Indian troops

CAPTURE OF MAFIA ISLAND—I

Mafia Island was German territory off the coast of German East Africa. East Indian troops are shown landing at Kissimani Beach. The English *sahib* is conspicuous as he stands in sun-helmet and spotless white uniform at the bow of the boat.

CAPTURE OF MAFIA ISLAND—II

The British flag is being hoisted at Utende, while the King's African Rifles surround it in hollow-square formation

GERMAN SOUTHWEST AFRICA CAMEL CORPS

At the beginning of the war British South Africa was invaded from German Southwest. But the Boers disappointed the Germans by remaining true to the British. Botha had fought against England in the Boer War, but he led the Boers against the Germans, and soon conquered German Southwest for the British Empire.

CAMELS EN ROUTE FOR PALESTINE

It is possible that the same animals may appear both in this picture and in the preceding one. For when the British conquered German Southwest Africa they would naturally have realized the potential value of the German trained camels in safeguarding Egypt, and, later, in the campaigns of Mesopotamia and Palestine.

FRENCH AFRICAN TROOPS AT DUALA—I

Machine gun drill at Duala barracks. As German Southwest Africa was exposed to assault from its more prosperous neighbour, British South Africa, so the (German) Kamerun was at the mercy of the French who were well established in the adjoining French Congo and Sudan. The British colonists in Nigeria and the Belgians in the Belgian Congo were other hostile neighbours.

FRENCH AFRICAN TROOPS AT DUALA—II

A practice march.

The German possessions in western equatorial Africa melted away before French-drilled and British-drilled troops like these, soon after the war began. "German Togoland was conquered by Anglo-French forces after a campaign which lasted but three weeks and was ended in August, 1914. On February 18 of the following year the Kamerun was also in British and French hands."

JAPAN STRIKES GERMANY AT KIAOU CHAU—I

Japanese artillerymen awaiting telephone orders from Headquarters before starting the bombardment of Tsing-tau. They were assisted in this bombardment by the Allied warships.

"Early in September (1914) a Japanese expedition, amounting to one strong division, was landed at Kiaou Chau. . . . Without haste and methodically the Japanese pushed their trenches forward and November 6 saw the forts of the German colony in ruin. The next day Tsing-tau surrendered."

JAPAN STRIKES GERMANY AT KIAOU CHAU—II

Part of the obstacles which a strong Japanese force found no difficulty in overcoming. The city of Tsing Tau was encircled by miles of this barbed wire entanglement

JAPAN STRIKES GERMANY AT KIAOU CHAU—III

The effect of the bombardment on the big guns of the German fortress

efforts in Africa with something between disdain and benevolence. Even a German colony extending from the Atlantic to the Pacific and including the Belgian and French Congos did not stir the Briton's pulse, nor did the covert menace to South Africa, for a single moment revealed to the whole world when the Kaiser sent his historic message to President Kruger, disturb the equanimity of a Liberal Ministry, little concerned with Imperial ambitions and convinced that Britain had already reached the point of satiation so far as overseas annexations were concerned. In Central Africa, as in Asia Minor, the British Government and public of 1914 were reconciled to German development, provided it did not threaten the legitimate interests of France or precipitate any European conflict.

And it was this dream of a great African Empire, of a German Congo become almost as real as the German Rhine, of a German Tanganyika, of a Transafrican Empire, which was extinguished—for the period of the war at least—in the first months of the conflict and at the very hour when German victories in Europe filled the bulletins of the world. Thus the Hohenzollerns in their turn fared as had the House of Bourbon when at last sea power was roused.

### IV.  JAPAN

In the story of the extinction of German colonial power the Chinese incident naturally takes first place, not merely because it happened to be chronologically the first, but because the participation of Japan gave it unusual value and raised questions which may have incalculable importance in the future, both in the Far East and for the United States and the British colonies of the Australian and American continents.

By her treaty with Britain, by the terms of the alliance that followed the Russo-Japanese War, Japan was bound to support Britain east of Suez, so her participation in attack upon Kiaou-Chau was always assured. Yet there were deeper reasons which made the war popular in the Japanese mind. Following the war with China and after a sweeping victory, German intervention had denied Japan the harvest her victories had earned and her rulers demanded. At this moment in

Far Eastern history, Germany played the part she had played at Berlin. Then she had vetoed Russian aspirations at the Dardanelles. In the later episode she barred the Japanese route to equally cherished objectives and made herself the spokesman for Europe. Here was an injury which the Japanese never forgave, although at the moment they were powerless to revenge.

Not less an affront to Japanese pride was the constantly repeated appeal of the German Emperor to the Western nations to unite in a crusade against "the Yellow Peril." The words of the Emperor when he sent a German expedition to Pekin, exhorting his troops to remember the deeds of Attila and emulate them—an exhortation faithfully observed and remembered in later days when German armies in Belgium and France outstripped the Huns of Attila in destruction—and the attack upon the "Yellow race" therein contained, were a memorable affront to a proud nation, conscious of its growing power and its great achievement, already rivalling the Western races in its development, commercial and industrial, and determined to take an equal rank amongst the great nations of the world.

Nor were these sentimental reasons alone of importance. The Far East, China, was the natural field for Japanese industrial and political expansion. The war with Russia had banished the Slav from the Korean Peninsula and gained both Southern Manchuria and Port Arthur. Having thrust one European nation out of China, Japan could with real enthusiasm aid in the expulsion of another. Nor was there any comparison between the Russian and the German in the matter of commercial rivalry. If Russia could be regarded as a future rival, when she had, in her time, become an industrial and manufacturing nation, Germany was already a real commercial rival. Russia lacked a commercial fleet, but already German ships sailed the Chinese waters and the German flag appeared ever more frequently in Chinese ports. Moreover, from Tsingtau a German railroad had already tapped the coal regions of Shantung, and Teutonic appetite for Chinese territory showed marked expansion.

When Germany, like Russia, was expelled from the Far East, while

Britain and France were occupied with a long war—for the Japanese were not in the dark as to the prospects of the western war—while the United States was still given over to pacifist dreams, unarmed and incapable of defending its colonies or, for that matter, its own Pacific Coast line, Japan might look forward to a long period of unchallenged supremacy in the Far East, and in this time she would be able, not alone to establish her influence in China, but, through her manufacture of war materials for the Russians, acquire that capital she lacked and restore her finances shaken so severely by her war with Russia.

On the other hand, to every suggestion that she send her armies to Europe, Japan was bound to return a polite but firm negative.  It was not her concern; it was obviously to her profit that the Western nations should cripple themselves by a long war and find their whole energy for years concentrated upon the European battlefield.  If the war ended in the exhaustion of all the contending nations, Japan, still strong in her military and naval establishment, still possessing a huge and well-equipped army, her finances restored and her situation in China fortified by long occupation, could well believe that her place in the world would be increased, her power expanded.  Such a struggle might bring her incalculable profit; it could not threaten her with any real danger.  Such was Japanese policy.

By contrast with the political aspects of Japanese participation in the war the military incidents at Kiaou-Chau were insignificant.  On August 15 Japan despatched an ultimatum to Germany, demanding the departure of German ships from Chinese waters and the transfer of Kiaou-Chau to Japan, as a first step in its return to Chinese control. The time limit fixed in the ultimatum was August 23 and on that day Japan declared war upon Germany.

Early in September a Japanese expedition, amounting to one strong division, was landed near Kiaou-Chau.  Fifteen hundred British troops presently joined the Japanese, warships belonging to the Allied nations covered the transport operations and opened the bombardment of Tsingtau.  Without haste and methodically the Japanese pushed their trenches forward and November 6 saw the forts of the German colony in ruin.  The next day, November 7, Tsingtau surrendered.  A garrison of less than four thousand had made a brave but unavailing resistance. At the moment the German failure at Ypres was assured and the road to Calais barred, Berlin heard through enemy proclamations that her Far Eastern colony was lost.

In this same time Japanese warships had seized German islands in the Pacific, New Zealanders had occupied Samoa, Australians had taken Kaiser Wilhelm's Land.  German rule in the Pacific had been abolished.

### V.  IN GERMAN AFRICA

The conquest of German Africa is interesting, in the larger view, solely because of the South African episode.  Hardly a decade had passed since British armies had at last extinguished Boer resistance in the two Afrikander republics.  Only eight years had elapsed since home rule had been granted to the conquered Boers and the Union of South Africa had become a fact.  In all German calculations there had been the expectation that at a German appeal, South Africa—Boer South Africa—would rise again and that the outbreak of the European War would be the signal for the end of British rule south of the equator.

That this did not happen was due to the genius of the British race in dealing with its colonies.  South Africa had been swiftly reconciled after having been ravaged by a long, bitter war.  Forty-four years after French defeat, forty-three years after the Treaty of Frankfort, the mass of the people of Alsace continued to resent German rule and remained loyal to France.  But in less than a fifth of this time the conquered Boers had been reconciled to the new condition.

When the war came it had its echoes in South Africa.  De Wet, one of the most famous of the Boer leaders, promptly raised the standard of revolt and to this some thousands of the old Boers flocked.  But the real power in South Africa was Louis Botha, the greatest of Boer generals in the previous war and now the first Prime Minister in the new colony. In the great crisis he never hesitated, and his influence was decisive.  The last days of October saw the outbreak of the rebellion; by December 1 the whole thing had been stamped out, De Wet was a prisoner, all the raiding bands, which never attained the importance of armies, had been dispersed or captured. South Africa had demonstrated its determination to remain under British rule.

The next step was inevitable. British South Africa had been invaded from German Southwest Africa; the adjoining German colony had been the base for conspiracy and the starting point of invasion. Now, just as the American colonists in the Eighteenth Century had shared with the British the task of expelling the French from Canada, the Boers followed Botha in the invasion of German Southwest Africa and the end was not long in coming. July, 1915, saw the surrender of the last German commander, German Southwest Africa passed to the control of the Union of South Africa. And just as the American colonists disclosed a determination that Quebec should not be returned to the French, the South Africans early proclaimed their annexation of German Southwest Africa as definitive.

Germany had reckoned on the disaffection of British colonies the world over. She had believed the war would cause the loosening of the bonds that held together the British Empire. The response of Canada had been heard in the Second Battle of Ypres, when the Canadians had saved the day in the great gas attack. Australia and New Zealand answered to the roll call on Gallipoli Peninsula and the story of the Anzacs had become a part of Imperial history when the South Africans completed their task of extinguishing German rule in South Africa and accepted as the next duty the invasion of German East Africa. No disappointment of all that Germany suffered was more real or more serious than that caused by the course of the British colonials. She had hoped to disrupt the British Empire, but before the first anniversary of the war was over it was plain that she had cemented it.

As for the other colonial incidents, they call for but passing mention. German Togoland was conquered by Anglo-French forces after a campaign which lasted but three weeks and was ended in August, 1914. On February 18 of the following year the Kamerun was also in British and French hands. Only German East Africa remained and this was able, because of its size and the problems of transport, to resist with ever-diminishing force until the fourth year of the struggle. But the resistance was always hopeless and, long before this time, restricted to inland districts removed from that great railroad which had been the life line of German plans in Central Africa.

And in this collapse of her overseas empire may be found one more incentive to Germany's military activity in the period we are now to examine. Since sea power had demonstrated her helplessness beyond the mainland; since her colonial establishments had disappeared; it was patent that if Germany were to have her place upon the map, a place commensurate with her real greatness, it must be sought where her armies could march and where British sea power could not reach. And this led inevitably to the great Pan-German dream, to *Mitteleuropa*, with its Asiatic extensions.

# CHAPTER FIVE

## SUBMARINES

### I
### THE GERMAN CASE

With her flag banished from the high seas, her seaborne commerce paralyzed, her colonies one by one being gathered in by British, Japanese, and French troops; with the prospect of a long war where she had expected a swift triumph; with the realization that the United States was becoming the arsenal and the granary of her enemies, the Germans, after their defeats at the Marne and in Belgium and those of their Austrian ally at Lemberg and in Galicia, were, in the closing months of 1914, brought face to face with a situation which, however much it might arouse their anger, demanded such attention as might abolish what was now a threat of ultimate defeat.

To meet sea power Germany had no fleet commensurate with the task, and the first months of the war demonstrated that she could not by submarine warfare so diminish the British Grand Fleet as to make a decisive victory at sea even remotely possible. Her dream of carrying the war into Britain by Zeppelins and by airplanes was presently to prove idle. Zeppelin fleets were, it is true, to arrive over London and deposit their burden of bombs, but the ensuing destruction was soon shown to be relatively insignificant, while each return of the German air fleets stimulated British volunteering, roused British spirit to new determination, and brought British appreciation of the character of the war to a still more dangerous clarity.

As the war progressed, it became quite clear that Admiral Mahan's dictum would be proven accurate and that the dominant sea power would rewrite the rules of international war governing blockades to suit its own necessity. Very early in the contest the British Government repudiated the agreements contained in the Declaration of London, never, be it said,

accepted by the British Government by any official act, although they
had been formulated in a conference which took place in the British
capital and had enlisted the support of British representatives at the
gathering.  Nor is it unworthy of note that, when the war came, Britain refused to follow the principles championed by her delegates at the
precise moment when Germany demanded that these same principles—
rejected by her delegates—should become the rules of marine conflict,
thus supplying one more example of the vagaries of diplomacy.

From the very start it became clear that British naval power would
more and more seek to seal up Germany, to interrupt the flow of food
and material, non-contraband as well as contraband, of wheat and
cotton as well as shells and copper.  Nor was it less clear that the British
naval policy, and in this policy all of the Allies concurred, would aim also
at shutting up those neutral doorways by which necessary food and
munitions could reach Germany, although this involved an actual, if
not a technical, blockade of the ports of Holland and the Scandinavian
countries and an ever-increasing interference with American trade on
the high seas.

How was Germany to deal with this problem which carried with it the
very real threat of ultimate privation for her people and of complete exhaustion of war material for her armies?  Should she seek to employ her
submarines against enemy and neutral marine alike and, by arousing
fear, forbid the use of European waters by neutral ships bearing food and
munitions to her foe and thus bring her enemies to terms by turning their
tactics against them?  Should she refrain from direct acts herself so far as
neutrals were concerned and await the very probable embroilment of the
neutrals with Great Britain and the subsequent action of the United
States to protect its overseas commerce from British interference?

Both policies had much to commend themselves to the German mind.
Immediate war upon all British shipping, passenger ships as well as
cargo boats, would bring the meaning of the struggle home to the sea-
faring nation of Britain.  It would abolish that intolerable situation in
which the mass of the British people were able to rest safe and secure on
their islands, while the threat of invasion and the peril of starvation over-

hung the German people. It would strike Britain at her most vital and sensitive point—her fleet, her merchant marine. More than this, it would rouse German confidence and German enthusiasm as nothing else could, for in the early months of the war the "Hymn of Hate" was on all lips and "Gott Strafe England" the most familiar of German salutations.

On the other hand, while such a course was calculated to injure Britain, it might conceivably rouse the neutrals. The United States might be driven to take steps against Germany and become a member of the alliance against her, while if Germany held her hand, all German representatives in America could, with reasonable accuracy, assure her that the American people, with the memories of 1812 still in mind, would not permit British fleets to bar their ships or their products from the European trade when these ships and these products were proceeding in strict conformity with international law. Moreover, even if the United States did not, in fact, declare war upon Britain because of British offending, there remained the possibility that she would embargo all war material destined for British and French armies and vital to their safety, to their existence. And, after all, this would mean the realization of the chief German purpose, for, deprived of this American aid, the Allied armies would almost inevitably fall to German arms.

## II. GERMAN POLICY

In this dilemma the German statesmen were not able early to adopt a definite policy. They could not decide at first upon an absolutely "ruthless" submarine war. They could not make up their minds to leave the initiative to Britain and await the eventual profit when American public opinion should be properly roused, as their agents and representatives were bound to arouse it. And in the end this faltering between two policies led to the failure of both. The history of the relations between America and Germany, growing out of the submarine controversy, belongs to that volume which will discuss America's entrance into the world conflict and there will be examined in detail, but it is appropriate now to examine the submarine question as it affected the war situation in the first eighteen months of the conflict.

With the coming of the New Year (1915) the British were moved to the first important step in the long series that led to ultimate rallying of the United States and many other neutrals to the Allied cause. Foreseeing the eventual shortage of food, the German Government, with a prevision strikingly contrasting with Allied blindness, ordered the organization within Germany of a sort of glorified trust, which, under Government authority, was to seize all the wheat in Germany and to regulate its distribution. Alleging that this warranted treating wheat as contraband, the British Government announced that it would henceforth adopt such a course and it fortified its decision by declaring that this policy was to be recognized also as a reprisal for German offences against international law.

To this Germany responded with her proclamation of a blockade of Britain to begin in February, a submarine blockade, further strengthened by the wholesale sowing of mines. She announced a policy of sowing mines within the waters of Britain, sinking belligerent merchantmen on sight, and warned neutrals against entering these waters lest they should be the victims of accidents. In this first declaration there was no suggestion of "ruthlessness" so far as neutral ships were concerned.

But such a policy not only did violence to all international law regulating blockades, but also was perilous alike to non-contraband goods of neutrals carried in belligerent bottoms and to the lives of American and other neutral citizens travelling upon passenger ships flying belligerent flags. In both cases, too, it was an invasion of the unquestioned rights of neutrals, although not more serious than certain British invasions, save in a single circumstance. It involved the lives of neutrals, whereas the British acts involved only property and even there left an opportunity for redress in British prize courts.

As between the sinking of belligerent merchant ships and passenger boats there was a distinction which might have been established in the neutral minds had Germany permitted the matter to await argument before going further. International law as it existed was based upon conditions that obtained in the Civil War era. Then the ability of the warship, having captured a prize, to take it to port; the opportunity for searching suspected merchantmen, and for manning them with prize crews were unmistakable. But between 1864 and 1914 a half century had elapsed, and the whole machinery of marine warfare had changed while the precepts of international law governing this warfare remained unmodified.

By Britain's blockade, which had taken on illegal features and was patently destined to transgress still further international law, the whole civilian population of Germany was threatened with starvation. In the submarine Germany possessed a weapon which might enable her to strike back. Was she estopped from using it because international law had been compiled before the submarine became a detail in war? That she should be prevented from employing this against belligerent merchantmen, despite the incidental added risk in the case of the crews of such vessels, was manifestly unfair. The submarine could not, like the old sailing ship of war or the steam craft of the Civil War period, put a prize crew aboard a merchantman; it could not take off the prize's crew because it had no room to house it. Moreover, it was itself in deadly peril, by reason of its fragility, if such merchant ships as crossed its pathway did as they were promptly to do, namely arm themselves with guns sufficiently powerful to dispose of a submarine.

Therefore, when Germany did actually put into practice her threatened policy in the matter of enemy merchant marine—as one distinguished British naval authority, Sir Percy Scott, in a memorable statement, had forecast before the war—there was no clear and immediate reaction in neutral nations. The solemn warning of the President of the United States, evoked by the Berlin proclamation of this "blockade" and indicative of a determination on the part of the American Government to defend the lives of its citizens and to hold Germany to "strict accountability" for any injury to American shipping, was not accepted in America as covering the case of British and French merchant ships. It was felt at once to be designed to meet the case of American ships and American sailors navigating them, and to belligerent passenger ships carrying American citizens to Europe, since the rapid decay of American merchant marine, due to unintelligent shipping laws, had almost compelled Americans having business in Europe to travel by foreign passenger craft, as the Germans themselves well knew.

And in the early days of this first submarine campaign, while merchant ships of the Allies were the sole victims and the Allied press was filled with denunciations of the Germans as pirates and murderers, American and other neutral opinion remained calm. Between the two belligerent principles, both illegal, both violating all the letter if not the spirit of international law, the neutrals did not feel themselves called upon to choose, and the United States signalized its attitude by addressing an identic note to Great Britain and to Germany protesting against injuries suffered at the hands of both.

So far then the German submarine campaign encountered no great obstacle, but, on the other hand, it accomplished no great result. Merchant ships were sunk, but not in impressive numbers. British sea-borne trade was not paralyzed. American munitions continued to pour into Britain and France, and Kitchener's new armies were in part equipped in America, while for France and England, America became the farm and the factory. More than this, the Germans could suspect a growing tendency in America, as the trade of the country with their enemies expanded, to endure hardships and wrongs incident to Allied policies, to permit Allied interference with German-American trade, when Allied-American trade was more and more occupying all the industrial establishments of the nation and promising profits beyond the dreams of avarice.

### III.  "RUTHLESSNESS"

In this posture Germany was led to an extension of her submarine policy which had fatal consequences. Always in the German mind there appears to linger the notion that it is possible to accomplish by terror what cannot be achieved by the more familiar and legitimate methods of international intercourse. Now it seems clear that the Germans concluded that by extending their submarine campaign to include all belligerent ships—there was still no direct suggestion of an attack upon neutral vessels—the results would terrify neutrals and above all Americans into submission to German will and bring them to the prohibition of trade with the Allies.

So far the Germans had found the neutral world resigned, if not complaisant, in the face of their invasion of neutral rights. Could they not expect that this temper would endure—since to the German mind it was due in no small degree to fear of German might—if their submarines attacking British passenger ships should demonstrate in a striking and unmistakable manner the reality of their submarine threat, now become a little discredited in neutral minds? And the sinking of a few passenger ships, of some great and famous boat, would it not have an effect upon public opinion not to be exaggerated, an effect well-nigh necessary in the dark moments before the great German victories of 1915 began?

The flaw in all this reasoning was in the inability of the German to recognize that while nations can submit to many injustices and permit many of their rights to be invaded, no nation, save in a condition of absolute helplessness, can endure the murder of its own citizens and take no step to check the policy which involves their murder.

That the United States would take any drastic step against Germany, as long as her aggressions were aimed only at belligerent merchant ships, was always unlikely. Even in the case of American ships there was a plain disposition to accept apology and indemnity, where the injury had been manifestly or even apparently the result of mistake and not of design. But never at any time was there any real possibility that the United States would permanently tolerate that its citizens, travelling in strict accordance with their rights, be murdered upon the high seas, even if as an alternative the United States had to enter the war. To something approaching piracy the American Government did submit, both in the case of Britain and of Germany, but to murder it could not submit, and when the Germans at last definitely adopted a policy of murder the United States entered the war.

The decision of the Germans in the matter of unrestrained submarine operations is one of the great incidents of the war. It takes rank with the invasion of Belgium.  It was born of similar ideas and it led to similar results.  The condition of modern land war, the development of French defence, had left Germany but one avenue of attack upon France promising swift victory, and she took it.  The invasion of Belgium made British entrance into the war certain.  British sea power left Germany but one weapon on the ocean—the submarine.  She took it, and, by employing it in a ruthless fashion, brought the United States and other neutrals actively into the war at the moment when a favourable peace was not beyond her reach, and war-weary Allied nations were only roused to new determination by the arrival of American ships and soldiers in France.

Like the invasion of Belgium, the first German submarine campaign, which covers the period we are to examine, failed to achieve its main purpose.  Had it been restricted to merchantmen it could not have succeeded at this stage, but there would have been a very real possibility that the United States might have come to grave disagreements with British sea power and even to the point of embargoing war munitions.  After the submarine policy had been expressed in the *Lusitania* Massacre there never was a chance of this, and the United States marched surely, if unwittingly, to the declaration of April 6, 1917.  But it is useful to recall that until this crime, German submarine warfare upon the merchant marine of belligerents failed to arouse American anger and seemed one of the injuries incident to a world conflict, which should be endured by a nation resolved to remain outside the struggle.  In the Napoleonic Wars both England and France behaved toward us even more outrageously than the Germans before the *Lusitania* crime, and between the German and Allied policies there was a difference in method rather than spirit, since both were equally regardless of international law and neutral rights.

IV.   AMERICA AND GERMANY

Between April, 1915, and February, 1916, the period in which the submarine played only a minor part, its depredations were not serious, its potentialities were hardly appreciated, and the British naval authorities were too easily satisfied by their apparent success in dealing with the menace.    Neither on land nor on sea was the effect of this new engine of real weight.

Yet the consequences of the unrestricted use of the submarine were ultimately to raise an issue between the United States and Germany which led to war.    When the year 1915 opened no man could safely forecast the ultimate course of American policy.    The British decision to forbid the transport of foodstuffs to German ports, announced in a decree of February 2, raised instant protest in America.    The German response of February 4, proclaiming the war zone, transformed the problem from a quarrel between America and the Allies to a dispute between the United States and both coalitions.    The Anglo-French response of March 1, which interdicted all seaborne commerce with Germany, temporarily gave to the Allies the larger share of American resentment.

It is only after the *Lusitania* Massacre of May 7 that the tide definitely turns in America, that the question at issue between the United States and Germany excludes from real discussion the disputes between the United States and the Allies.    After May 7 Germany becomes more and more involved, while the Allies are less and less impeded by American protest or American indignation.    Presently the whole question becomes German-American and the United States more and more assumes the position of insisting that Germany shall, no matter what the cost to herself, abandon a policy jeopardizing American lives and property.

All this belongs to the narrative of America's relation to the war. Yet it is essential to recognize that, in the period that we are to review now, Germany lost the chance of utilizing American insistence upon the rights of neutrals as a weapon to break down British blockade.    She lost it by her submarine campaign and she lost it forever by the *Lusitania* crime.    Her first submarine campaign thus cost her all hope of American aid, aid to come by an American defence of international law; her second submarine campaign led straight to war with America.

We know now that Germany was forced into the first campaign by Admiral Tirpitz and a few of his associates, who exaggerated the possible achievement of the submarine fleet.    We know now that wiser statesmen objected to the campaign, not because of any tenderness of heart, but because they believed the profit would not balance the loss, since the German submarine fleet was too small to obtain any real success. We know now that, in the end, in the spring of 1916, this unrestricted submarine warfare was abandoned temporarily, because it had been proved that Germany could not pursue it further without bringing the United States into the war and because at that date she had but few submarines available. Presently we shall see the British people and their naval authorities convinced that Germany had abandoned the first campaign because of the achievement of the British fleet, and had only used American dangers as a pretext, and later we shall see how mistaken were these Englishmen and how costly their complacency proved.

In the second phase of the war, German use of the submarine led to grave consequences without considerable profit. On the material side it insured to the Allies all the resources of American factories and mines, since it abolished all chance of an embargo following a dispute between Washington and London over patently illegal British use of sea power. On the moral side it transformed the character of the war in the neutral mind. Thus May 7, the morning of the *Lusitania* Massacre, is a date memorable in the history of the war; memorable therefore in all human history. Off Old Head of Kinsale, as before Liége, Germany invoked the law of necessity, and as the former crime roused Britain, the latter eventually stirred the United States.

Here, after all, is the real significance and the only actual achievement of the first submarine campaign. It did not bring Great Britain to her knees, as the violation of Belgian territory had not resulted in the destruction of France. It merely enlisted a new enemy where it sought to conquer an old antagonist. Again the greatest price of their "terribleness" was destined to be paid by Germans.

THE BURNING OF AN ALLIED FOOD SHIP

This steamer was set on fire by a German U-boat commander. The picture was reproduced from a German newspaper. It was part of the consistent German effort to cheer up the German people by attempting to prove to them the efficiency of the ruthless submarine campaign.

WHY U-BOAT COMMANDERS DO NOT ALWAYS REPORT—I

An interesting scene in the submarine drama as enacted in the Mediterranean. The ship from which the photograph was taken fired a shot at a German submarine. The shell is seen breaking over the spot where the U-boat submerged. A French hydroplane and a submarine chaser are manoeuvring for an attack on her in case she reappears.

WHY U-BOAT COMMANDERS DO NOT ALWAYS REPORT—II

A disabled German submarine which was cast ashore, and broke her back on the French side of the Straits of Dover

U-BOAT INTERIORS—I

Cross-section of a German submarine captured at Pas-de-Calais. She is far more comfortable and less crowded than the mine-layer shown on the opposite page

U-BOAT INTERIORS—II   Captured by the British navy in the English Channel, she was loaned to the United States for use in the Second Liberty Loan Campaign.   She was cut into three sections and carried across the Atlantic on a steamer.   On her arrival at New York, she was set up in Central Park for the inspection of prospective buyers of Liberty Bonds.

The densely packed interior of the German submarine mine-layer *U. C. 5*

AN ENGLISH SUBMARINE

She is running high in the water, with practically all her crew on deck and in the conning-tower

THE GERMAN SUBMARINE MINE-LAYER *U. C. 5*

A cross-section of the interior of this vessel may be seen on the preceding page. Two mines are visible on her deck in this picture. She can carry twelve more in the six tubes in her forward hold, as shown in the other picture

KING GEORGE INSPECTS A BRITISH SUBMARINE

The sea is rough and the King is feeling cautiously for the top step of the companion ladder

A SUBMARINE IN A SEAWAY

Looking aft from the conning-tower of a British U-boat in the North Sea, where it is often rough going for submarines travelling on the surface

A BRITISH SUBMARINE THAT PASSED THE DARDANELLES MINES

The crew of the British *E 11* are being cheered by comrades on another British vessel, as the *E 11* returns from a venture into the mine-strewn waters of the Dardanelles

# CHAPTER SIX

## THE BATTLE OF THE DUNAJEC

### I

### THE EASTERN SITUATION

On May Day, 1915, a huge German army under Field Marshal von Mackensen attacked the Russian army commanded by a Bulgarian general, Radko Dimitrieff, and standing between the Dunajec and Biala rivers, some thirty miles east of Cracow, well-nigh destroyed it and began that long offensive which was not to end until German armies had penetrated deeply into Russian territory, taken Warsaw and Brest-Litovsk, and temporarily paralyzed Russian military power.

The Battle of the Dunajec is the second of the great conflicts of the war—the Marne, the Dunajec, and Verdun. These are the great struggles of the first three years and in many respects the Dunajec must rank after the Marne, while viewed from the standpoint of the present hour it seems certain to prove one of the truly decisive battles of human history, for by this disaster were sown the seeds of that Russian Revolution which was to come less than two years later. It marked the decisive step toward the overthrow of the Romanoff dynasty and the consequent total transformation of the character and prospects of the war on the eastern front and, in a sense, of the whole war. Just as the Battle of the Marne supplies the central unity of the first phase of the war, the Dunajec furnishes the same central point for the second. All the campaigns and all the important developments derive their chief significance from this great struggle, which (so remote did the Galician field seem to the world at the moment) appeared insignificant beside the barren trench struggles about the ruins of Ypres.

The conditions under which this battle were fought are simply told. From the Battle of Lemberg onward Germany had sought steadily to bolster up the shaken Austrian armies. She had endeavoured by one costly offensive after another, directed at Warsaw from her own territory, to relieve the pressure upon her ally, throw the Russians back behind the middle Vistula and the Niemen, and compel them to give over their great effort to crush Austria.   None of these efforts had been a complete success nor yet a total failure.   The victories of Hindenburg at Tannenberg and the Masurian Lakes had taken a terrible toll of Russian troops.   Russian victories over the Austrians at Lemberg and afterward just missed dealing the final blow to the Hapsburg armies because of German aid promptly given and efficiently administered.

But long before spring came the Germans had recognized that it was no longer possible to save Austria by offensives directed from Breslau, Posen, or East Prussia upon Warsaw.   They had perceived, too, that it was not going to be possible to renew their bid for a decision in the west until they had settled with Russia by inflicting a sweeping and complete defeat upon the Czar's armies, which should eliminate them from the reckoning and might procure a separate peace by producing such a revolution within Russia as would dispose of the Slav enemy for the duration of the war.   At the least they were now determined to drive the Russian armies from Austrian territory and so disorganize their military establishment as to gain time and opportunity to go west again.

Having resolved that their major campaign for 1915 should be made in the east the Germans had to decide at what point they would make their main offensive.   The failures along the Niemen-Narew-Bobr line from Grodno to the Vistula, the bloody repulses on the Bzura-Rawka front, had exhausted the possibilities on the north and in the centre. Despite all efforts, these attacks had been repulsed and Russian pressure upon Austria had continued.   Nor was there a more shining opportunity to be found far to the south on the Rumanian frontier.   To attack here was still to permit the Russian pressure, the main thrust at Hungary, to continue.   Equally unattractive was the front along the Carpathians, for here the Russians, even were they driven back, would be able to maintain a long and costly defence in the Dukla and Lupkow Passes, possessing communications behind them and already holding the crests of the range along the portion of the mountain front which was available for operations.

The decision of the Germans was therefore for the front between the Carpathians and the Vistula, where the Russian line, having made the great "elbow" west of the Dukla Pass, ran straight to the north. Could they break the Russian line here, the Germans would threaten the rear and communications of the armies fighting along the Carpathians, particularly that of Brusiloff. Here they might hope to achieve, as they did in fact almost achieve, another Sedan, but they could be assured that in any event a successful penetration of the Dunajec line would cause the collapse of the whole Russian front from the upper Vistula to Rumania, with the consequent liberation of most of Galicia.

## II.   GERMAN TACTICS

The method by which the German sought to attain his goal is of supreme interest because it reveals a new form of warfare. It was repeated in every detail at Verdun and in a modified form at the Somme, and an examination of the system sheds invaluable light on the later struggle. It represented the application of new weapons and new discoveries to the art of war and it is a landmark in military history, on the scientific side. All the battles that came after this struggle for the next two and a half years were in the main of the same type.

At Neuve Chapelle Field Marshal Sir John French had almost achieved a major success, the actual breaking of the German line by means of massed artillery bombardment. On a front of less than a mile he had concentrated three hundred guns. The storm from this artillery, the "drum fire" of this unprecedented concentration, had swept away the German trenches and the German barbed wire. The road to Lille had been open for hours after this tornado of shells and it was the failure of reserves to arrive that had spoiled the best chance the Allies were to have for more than two years to break the German line from Switzerland to the sea.

The method of French was now adopted by Mackensen, but it was magnified to colossal proportions. In place of three hundred guns, the

Germans transported to western Galicia not less than two thousand, many of them of the heaviest calibre, and behind them they massed a head of shells previously unprecedented in war.    What Sir John French had done to a mile of German front in Flanders, Mackensen now purposed to do to many miles of the Russian front.    Nor was this all.    Having broken the lines before him he purposed, still moving his heavy artillery forward, to continue to break down and destroy each successive line on which the Russians might rally.    He had thus fashioned a mobile battering ram.

And behind the ram were many corps of the best German troops. For this campaign the pick of German first-line troops had been selected. The army that Mackensen commanded was probably, given its size, the best army that Germany had put into the field, for despite heavy losses her military machine had not yet begun to break down through wastage of its officers and annihilation of its youth.

The mission of this army of attack, Mackensen's "phalanx" as it presently came to be described, was to finish the work begun by the guns, to stamp out the last feeble resistance, and sweep on as a wave might rush through a dike already undermined by dynamite.    There was no intention that this army should extend its front; it had no part in the work of the flanks; it had no part in the work of the regular forces holding the line before it attacked.    Its mission was to batter its way, steadily, irresistibly, through the Russian positions, always attacking on the narrow front which could be prepared by the guns.

The effect of this strategy is easy to grasp.    Right and left of the sector attacked Russian armies stood firm, even took the offensive, but the Russians could not concentrate guns or munitions to meet this main thrust and each time they endeavoured to stand before it their line was crumpled up under the storm of shells that fell upon it.    And when this line had crumpled, the "phalanx" pushed through and opened a new breach, which compelled a reorganization of all the Russian front to conform to the retreat of the army which yielded to the main German thrust.

Time and again Russian armies north and south of Mackensen's

**THE RUSSIAN FRONT WHEN THE DUNAJEC BEGAN**

*White arrow* shows the point chosen by Mackensen for the attack of his mobile battering-ram

operative front swept forward, defeated and drove German and
Austrian troops, winning victories of considerable magnitude, taking
thousands of prisoners, but always on the morrow of such successes they
were faced with the fact that this Mackensen "phalanx" had pushed
forward over another barrier, broken the Russian centre between the
mountains and the Vistula at a new point, and the wings had to retire
to keep their alignment with the centre.

Actually there was something glacierlike in this German advance.
It was necessarily slow, because the guns could only move short distances
in any day, and the transport of munitions became more and more difficult as the Russians destroyed the roads and bridges, but it was always
irresistible, it was always beyond Russian resources to halt it, until the
hour when it passed the Russian frontier and reached a region destitute
alike of good roads and good railroads; then it came to a halt of a necessity.   But by this time its work had been done and the task that remained fell to other armies and in another field.

### III.   THE GREAT BLOW

When the great blow fell the position of three Russian armies immediately affected was this:  North of the Vistula the army of General
Evarts stood behind the Nida River, which enters the Vistula from the
north near the point where the Dunajec flows in from the south.   His
troops had enjoyed quiet for a long time and had no further mission at
the moment than to hold the sector entrusted to them.   South of the Vistula was the army of Dimitrieff, standing behind the Dunajec before
Tarnow and thence behind the Biala, right down to the Carpathians.
It, too, was charged with a defensive mission merely.   The army of
Brusiloff, which made junction with Dimitrieff's in the foothills of the
Carpathians, faced south, not west as did the other two, and was fighting
its way into Hungary.   It had forced the Dukla and Lupkow passes and
its victorious troops were already almost within sight of the Hungarian
plain.   This army was the hammer of the Russian military establishment,
and Allied capitals all too easily believed that, since it had now passed
the crests of the range, the road to Budapest and Vienna lay open to it.

Przemysl had fallen on March 22; the Russian troops which had thus been released had in the main been sent to Brusiloff, and on May 1 he was still advancing; his army was still victorious, yet it was possible to detect a slowing down. Russian progression in the Battle of the Carpathians was never actually ended until the Battle of the Dunajec

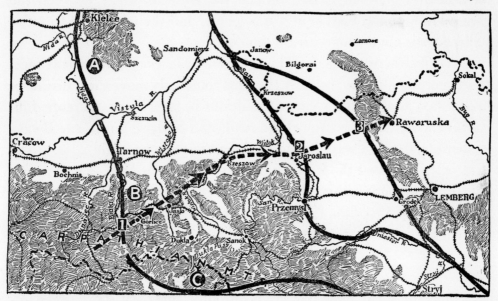

THE BATTLE OF THE DUNAJEC, MAY, 1915

*A* shows position of General Evarts north of the Vistula.
*B* shows where Dimitrieff's army was practically destroyed by Mackensen's "phalanx."
*C* shows position of Brusiloff's army which just managed to escape destruction.
*Lines* 1, 2, and 3 show the positions successively occupied by the Russians; and the *dotted line* shows the resistless advance of Mackensen's "phalanx."

compelled Brusiloff to flee a field of victory to escape ruin in consequence of disaster elsewhere, and yet the strain upon Russia of eight months of campaign had been tremendous; Russian supplies of munitions were already beginning to dry up and were presently to fail at the crucial moment.

At first only Dimitrieff's army was involved in the German attack. Its position was exceedingly good. It had before it the Dunajec River and then the Biala, an affluent coming down out of the mountains. Both streams were in flood as a result of spring thaws. The lines had been very thoroughly fortified and had withstood heavy attacks in the past. Indeed, so successfully had they withstood attack that Dimitrieff had been led into a fatal error and had prepared no positions to the rear, although the Wislok and the Wistok rivers, behind him, offered equally good fronts on which to withstand German attack if the Dunajec line should be forced.

Despite the belief at the time, the Russian army at the Dunajec was by no means lacking either in munitions or guns.   It had the fair allowance of a Russian army, but this allowance was totally inadequate to face the German concentration.   In addition, Dimitrieff had behind him admirable railroad and highway lines.   Two trunk lines, one connecting Cracow with Lemberg via Tarnow, the other running from Gorlice to Stryj, supplied his rear.   No position of the whole Russian front seemed in the closing days of April, 1915, better calculated to hold, and no general had a better reputation than the soldier who had broken Turkish armies at Lule Burgas and won new laurels in the Lemberg campaign.

Yet on May Day this army was almost totally destroyed by the first German attack.   The Teutonic artillery had been concentrated before Gorlice, which, for the Germans, gives its name to the battle. Under a bombardment estimated to have consumed 700,000 shells the whole Russian lines of defence collapsed, the trenches were levelled, the barbed-wire entanglements destroyed; under the terrible shell-fire the Russian troops died in great numbers.   Their resistance was not merely broken—it was destroyed—and at the end of the first day Dimitrieff's army had almost ceased to exist.   Only broken detachments were flowing back eastward toward the Wislok.   The road was open to Mackensen's "phalanx" and the German infantry, passing to the offensive, forded the Biala and pressed forward.

Was the German attack a surprise?   In the main there can be no doubt of it.   It was a surprise as Verdun was a surprise.   In Galicia, as later in Lorraine, Allied observers had reported German activity. There was a general suspicion that a heavy blow was to fall, but the true magnitude of the blow was not foreseen, could not be foreseen. When it fell it tore the Russian defence into ribbons, just as the later attack tore the French line from Brabant to Ornes into ribbons.   On

May 2 and 3 the Russian army was in precisely the state of the French army on February 23 and 24 a year later.   Fortunately for France she was able to make a new concentration of men and guns a few miles behind the shattered front and pin down the German advance, thus localizing the struggle to the Verdun sector.   This the Russians could not do, and, as a consequence, the effect rapidly extended to adjoining armies.

#### IV.   BRUSILOFF ESCAPES

The position of Brusiloff's army now became one of extreme peril. The collapse of Dimitrieff's army had exposed his flank and rear; the victorious Germans were nearer to his lines of communication than were his main forces, which were far south of the Carpathians.   And the German advance was moving rapidly across his rear with the clear purpose to seize these lines of communication and thus encircle him, throwing Mackensen's forces to his rear, while the armies before him in the Carpathians passed to the attack to hold his troops on their front.   Yet Brusiloff did escape and his escape is as brilliant as the similar manœuvre of Kluck before Paris, when the German general slipped away from the British and brought his troops back to parry and beat down the deadly thrust of the French north of the Marne and west of the Ourcq.

Had Dimitrieff taken the trouble to prepare a line behind him at the Wislok, there would have been no great danger to Brusiloff and his retreat might have been deliberate, although there is little reason to believe that the Russians could have fought more than a delaying fight at this stream, for the German artillery concentration was too overwhelming to allow sustained resistance by an army as hopelessly outgunned as the Russian.   On May 7 the German advance passed the Wislok at the important railroad junction of Jaslo.   The next day the Germans were across the Wistok, another river coming north out of the Carpathians parallel to the Dunajec and the Wislok and again offering an advantageous defensive position, had the Russians guarded against defeat.   As it was there was little defence, for there were no trench lines.

Brusiloff was now all but enveloped.   His position had been a salient at the start and the Germans were almost across the neck of the loop.

He was saved because Russian reserves, concentrated at Przemysl, were pushed out along the upper Wistok and succeeded in halting the German drive for a few hours.   This gave Brusiloff just time to slip out of the rapidly tightening noose.   He did not get all his troops away; a division was caught, many guns and men were lost; but by May 12 his main forces were behind the San, and the Russian front had been restored. It had been restored in the sense that thenceforth the Germans were to face organized resistance—the days after Dimitrieff's collapse, when they had no real organized force before them, were over.   So also was the chance of a supreme success, the capture of the Russian armies in the Carpathians.   Only once more, this time at Vilna, were the Russians to face as terrible a danger, and there their escape was much easier.

The end of the second week in May then sees the Russian armies once more in line. Evarts has retired from the Nida to conform to the retreat south of the Vistula.   Dimitrieff's army has ceased to exist, but a new army is in position from the Vistula along the San through Jaroslav and Przemysl to the Carpathians.

On this front was fought the Battle of the San, which was a final effort of the Russians to beat down the German thrust, as they had beaten down an Austrian thrust on the same front in the previous year. But the effort was vain.   Mackensen had moved his "phalanx" north-eastward along the railroad from Gorlice to Jaslo and from Jaslo to Rzeszow, where the branch line joined the main Lemberg-Cracow trunk line.   He now forced the passage of the San at Jaroslav and by forcing the line of the San compelled a new Russian retreat, this time to the very gates of Lemberg, to the famous Grodek line, a system of lakes and marshes a few miles west of the Galician capital.

Meantime the Austro-German army, which had been holding Brusi-loff in the Carpathians, pushed north and struck in the rear of Przemysl, seeking to encircle it from the south, as Mackensen, having passed the San, aimed at encircling it from the north.   In the face of this double thrust the Russians clung to Przemysl until June 2, always, however, with the clear recognition that it must ultimately be abandoned.   Six weeks after this stronghold had fallen to Russian arms a Bavarian contingent entered the town, on the heels of the Russian troops who just slipped between the sides of the closing neck of the salient and took the road to Lemberg.

Meantime, counter-offensives, by Evarts north of the Vistula and by Lechitsky on the front of Bukovina, had won smart local successes, but despite large captures of prisoners these operations could not influence the main campaign. The first days of June saw the Russians standing north of the Dniester and east of the Grodek Lakes. All of western Galicia had been lost and German troops were already across the Russian frontier east of the San. The Galician campaign was entering its last phase.

### V. LEMBERG

In the Grodek line the Russians occupied the last defensive line covering Lemberg. Of itself the position was impregnable and their southern flank was securely posted behind the Dneister. But if the artillery of Mackensen could not penetrate the swamps and marshes of the Grodek region, there was open to them a road by which they might turn them. Northward from Jaroslav to Rawa Russka ran the railroad down which Russky had come in his great attack of September, 1914. He had turned the Grodek line by coming round the northern end of the swampy country and defeating the Austrians at Rawa Russka. Once he had won a victory about this town, the Austrians had to fall back behind the San.

Mackensen simply reversed the proceeding. He moved from Jaroslav north to Rawa Russka, defeated the Russian troops there by means of his heavy artillery, and then began to turn south toward Lemberg and across the rear of the Russian armies. The threat was sufficient. June 22 the Russian armies left the Galician capital, which they had occupied since the first days of September, 1914. All the vast railroad network was restored to Austrian hands. Galicia was reconquered save for a small strip in the east. First taking up their position behind the Gnila Lipa, the line on which the Austrians had defended Lemberg in the previous year, the Russians presently withdrew behind the Zlota Lipa and then to the Sereth, where at last their retreat in Galicia came to an end.

Thus, in a campaign of less than eight weeks, Germany had freed Galicia. She had retaken more than 30,000 square miles of territory, with all their valuable oil wells and railroad lines. She had deprived Russia of the fruits of eight months of effort. She had destroyed one Russian army and disorganized three. She had abolished the threat to Austria and regained the offensive in the east. The consequences of Austrian defeat at Lemberg in August and September, 1914, ceased to dictate eastern operations. Austria was saved. Russia was now endangered and the campaign in the east had only begun.

Actually the German operation had restored the condition on the eastern front that had existed in the first days of the war. The Warsaw salient, abolished by Russian advance in Galicia, was as it had been when Austria had launched her first blow toward Lublin. The Russians were now in the posture they had foreseen before the war, when they had planned to evacuate Poland and begin their fight along the Bug, a plan temporarily discarded when Germany decided to go west and left to Austria the task of disposing of Russian attacks until German armies had entered Paris and crushed France.

The situation of the Central Powers, however, was vastly different from that of August, 1914. Now Germany had great armies in the east, while on the west she was simply seeking to hold her lines and for this utilizing her great superiority in heavy artillery and machine guns. Now that Mackensen had cleared Galicia, Hindenburg was in a position from which he could assail the Warsaw salient north and south simultaneously and at the same time continue pressure at the centre between Warsaw and Ivangorod.

In the previous year Russia had been able to put good armies in the field reasonably well equipped for a short campaign. But ten months of battle had weakened these armies; their supplies of munitions were rapidly diminishing; there were lacking guns and equipment for new troops ready to take their place in line. In fact, Warsaw and Brest-Litovsk were already doomed and a Russian collapse was to be prevented now only if France and Britain, by attacks on the west front, could divert German guns and German troops to Artois or Champagne in such numbers as to give the Russians a breathing spell. Only this intervention could deprive Germany of the opportunity to harvest the fruits of her great success, and since no such intervention was possible, the tide of German success was to continue uninterrupted for many months.

The Dunajec was therefore the second of the great battles of the war and one of the memorable contests in all military history. It was a Napoleonic triumph in its proportions and in its conception. It must rank in German military history with Tannenberg. The one saved Prussia; the other first rescued Austria, threatened with invasion and destruction, then brought Russia to the point of collapse and then to revolution. Whatever the final outcome of the war, its effect upon eastern Europe was bound to be decisive. For the House of Romanoff, the Dunajec was as fatal as Leipzig proved for the First Napoleon.

# CHAPTER SEVEN

## ITALY DECIDES

### I

#### 1813–1915

On the morrow of his victories of Lutzen and Bautzen in 1813, Napoleon found himself confronted by a new antagonist. While the French Emperor was still successful in Silesia and Saxony, Austria joined the coalition fighting him. At the moment when their victorious armies were approaching Lemberg, the same thing now happened to Germany and Austria. At the most favourable hour in the conflict since the defeat at the Marne, the Central Powers were confronted by the Italian declaration of war—a declaration directed only at Austria-Hungary, to be sure, but bound to be extended in time to include Germany and, since the fate of Germany was now so inextricably bound up with that of Austria, having the actual effect of a declaration of war upon both Hohenzollern and Hapsburg Empires.

The decision of Italy proceeded from the mass of the people, "from the street," to use the contemptuous phrase of Prince von Bülow, describing the tumultuous crowds which, in the last days of May, 1915, thronged the streets of Milan, of Florence, of Rome itself, clamouring for war against the ancient oppressor of all Italy and against the dynasty which still held under its heavy hand the Italia Irredenta—Trieste and the Trentino. It was the millions who decided the course of Italy in May. Yet these millions after all were but following the course which clear-visioned statesmen had already foreseen. D'Annunzio, hailed by the masses, speaking in terms approaching lyric frenzy as he denounced the "traitors" to Italy who opposed Italian intervention, had but adopted the course which Sonnino, the Prime Minister, after calm reflection and cold judgment, had determined was the only possible course for Italy.

Like Austria in 1813, Italy in 1915 looked out upon a Europe which was bound to be remade as a consequence of the great struggle that was being waged. Should Italy remain neutral only a drawn battle could save her from actual injury. No matter which of the groups of powers won the war, a neutral Italy would suffer, for if the Allies triumphed, Slav and Greek states, enormously magnified, might occupy the eastern shore of the Adriatic from the Julian Alps to the Strait of Otranto, while if the Central Powers were victorious, Austria would descend to Salonica and Germany occupy Asiatic Turkey as a detail in the Teutonic dream of Mitteleuropa.

From the first days of the conflict—when the proclamation of Italian neutrality permitted the French to withdraw their troops from the Italian frontier, move their garrisons from North Africa and gather up the armies which were just strong enough, given all these advantages, to check the German advance at the Marne—Italy was bound to choose between the two great groups. Permanent neutrality was impossible, save only if the prospect that a victory would escape both contestants should be unmistakable. Nor was there ever any real hope that Italy could with profit to herself play the rôle described by a witty Frenchman as "rushing to the succour of the victor."

And by May, 1915, it was clear that the prospect of a drawn battle was still absent. Fortune had changed and was to change again. Before the Marne a German victory seemed assured. After the close of the western campaign and the concentration of world interest on the eastern front, Austrian defeats suggested a collapse in the Hapsburg Empire. Russia, victorious for the moment, began to discuss the erection along the Adriatic shores of a Jugo-Slavic state, which would include Serbia, Montenegro, Dalmatia, Croatia, and the Istrian shores.

While the war went on, while the decision was still doubtful, both groups of powers were bound to bid for Italian aid, to offer a considerable price, because between the two groups Italy now held the balance of power, but once peace had been restored and the victorious alliance had established its success beyond challenge, it would have no need to consult Italy in drawing its peace terms and no reason to fear an Italian challenge wherever these terms interfered with Italian aspirations.

London and Paris saw this fact only vaguely; the mass of the Italian people did not perceive it at all. Their emotions were roused by ancient wrongs and contemporary grievances. Above all, the intellectual element, the party of youth, was stirred by the fact that, while Italy's unredeemed lands still beckoned, while opportunity to acquire Trieste and the Trentino became more splendid each day, German agents and German representatives, having corrupted Italian politicians and laid hands upon Italian finance and industry, mobilized public men and influential journals in the Peninsula in support of that neutrality which involved the sacrifice of Italian aspirations to German purposes.

In the end the Italian decision was made in an hour of passion hardly to be paralleled in modern history. A Parliament, controlled by corrupt and bureaucratic tools of Germany; a Crown, reluctant to enter a war against a fellow sovereign who had been, until yesterday, an ally and a friend, were swept out of the pathway. Yet when the passion had died away, when the war became a grim and unromantic business and the examination of the Italian decision in the light of sober and matured judgment was made, it was perceived that no other decision had ever been possible and it was recognized that, for once at least, the people had been wiser than many of their leaders and the instinct of a race had asserted itself in wise opposition to the representatives of the people who sat on the Capitoline Hill.

## II.   YOUNG ITALY

Young Italy of the first years of the Twentieth Century had certain definite aims and aspirations. These were the aspirations of a people, long the subjects of brutal and selfish foreign tyranny, tardily come to independence, and now, after sombre years of domestic hardship and self-discipline, arrived at the point from which they believed they could undertake to achieve for their country abroad a rank to which its population, position, and recent progress gave it title.

In the generation that lay between the occupation of Rome and the close of the last century Italy had time and again seen her position in the world made humiliating through her inability to urge her own claims with more than passive earnestness.    France had shouldered her out of Tunis.    Austria had annexed Bosnia.    Britain had laid hands upon Egypt and Cyprus and was transforming the Mediterranean into a British lake.    Within the Triple Alliance Italy was treated rather as a poor relative than as an equal.    Outside of the Alliance, France and Russia, indignant at Italian presence in a hostile group, treated Italian policies and Italian aspirations with contemptuous hostility.

In Abyssinia an Italian effort to erect a colonial empire had met with terrible disaster and Adowa had been a demonstration for Europe of Italian military weakness.    Poverty and misery at home, a feeble foreign policy, and an abject subservience to German dictation, this had been the history of Italian affairs from the moment when unity was achieved to the hour when a new century was to usher in a new and for the Italian patriots a happier age.

Looking at the first years of this century it is possible to detect unmistakable evidence of another "*risorgimento*," a new stirring of old dreams, a growing determination to transform the world view of Italy as a museum and a repository of artistic splendour into a recognition of Italy as a virile and contemporary fact in a world of realities.    Like Germany, Italy was seeking her "place in the sun"; like Germany, Italy, the Young Italy which was rising, felt a sense of wrong, of shame, in the fact that its country was still great only in their dreams and that its influence was restricted, while more fortunate rivals continued to paint their colours on the maps of Asia and Africa and lay the foundations for future greatness beyond the narrow limits of Europe.

This Young Italy was, in its first days, neither hostile to Germany nor friendly with the enemies of Germany.    It was neither Germanophile nor Francophile; it was not even Anglophile as the Young Italy of Mazzini had been.    It was intensely national and it dreamed of attaining national objects, whether by alliance with Germany or with France it did not matter.    Another generation had won Piedmont with French aid and Venetia with Prussian.    The same realistic spirit stirred in the later generation.

Yet when this Young Italy faced the question of how it could attain its objectives it was clear from the outset that Austria-Hungary must first be removed from the pathway.    Whatever else Italy dreamed of— and the group of nationalists who were rising to influence had far-shining visions—it was essential first of all to achieve security at home by possessing the Trentino gateway to the northern plain.    Garibaldi in 1866 had invaded the Trentino and looked down upon Trent from the hills, but had been recalled by a timid government.    Bismarck had given scant hearing and no comfort to his ally when, after Sadowa, Italy had asked for the restoration of the frontier fixed by Napoleon for his Kingdom of Italy, the frontier which would give to Italy the gateway to her own lands, the gateway by which invasions, from time imme-morial, had descended from the Brenner Pass to the Venetian plain.

Nor did the possession of Trent complete the programme of Young Italy for unifying Italy.    Across the Isonzo, in the city of Trieste, more than 120,000 Italians were subjected to a brutal and stupid tyranny. Fearful of eventual Italian advance, Austria had sought to destroy Italian claims by submerging Italian-speaking populations in the flood of Slav immigrants who, led by official suggestion and invitation, de-scended from the mountains and in ever-growing numbers settled in Trieste and in Istria.    In the same fashion German-speaking settlers were thrust into the Italian communities of the Trentino.    Thus, pre-cisely as Germany by her stupid and harsh procedure in Alsace-Lorraine kept this question always before the world, always in the news of the day for the Frenchman, Austrian cruelty and oppression multiplied these "incidents" by which Italians were constantly reminded of their brethren beyond their frontiers, who still paid that price for race loyalty which had been demanded of Italians in Venice and Milan half a century before.

And as the Pan-German in Prussia did not limit his aspirations to the liberation of German populations beyond his frontiers but also turned his eyes toward regions once included in the German Empires of the past but inhabited by other races than the German and now destitute of all ambition to become German, Young Italy looked southward from Venice along the Dalmatian coast where the ruins of Roman baths flanked the palaces of Venetian governors, and thence toward the Near East, in whose waters Venice had been supreme and along whose shores Rome had once ruled unchallenged.

French supremacy in North Africa from the Syrtes to the Pillars of Hercules Young Italy had accepted, reserving Tripoli for their share— their meagre share of what had been one of the fairest fields of Roman colonization—but toward the Ægean, toward Asia Minor, toward Smyrna and Alexandretta, the new generation of Italian patriots looked with undisguised ambition. To make the Adriatic an Italian lake, to hold its ports, still bearing Italian names even on that east coast where the Slav wave was more and more submerging the Italian tongue, from Trieste to Valona, this was the dream of the Young Italy which was rising, which was now making its voice heard.

But all such aspirations encountered the ancient enemy in a new position. The House of Hapsburg, pushed back from the Mincio and the Adda, from the old Quadrilateral of Peschiera, Mantua, Verona, and Legnago, still clung to Riva and Trent, Gorizia and Gradisca; still held the eastward gateway between the Julian Alps and the Gulf of Trieste and the southern sallyport of Teutonism, between the Brenner Pass and the upper reaches of Lago de Garda. Vienna, too, was nourishing a dream of a southward march, by the Vardar Valley to Salonica, by the Morava route to the Golden Horn and thence to the Near East by the Hellespont. And behind this Austrian dream, beyond the Hapsburg capacity to realize unaided were the German hand and the German voice, which had bidden Italy abandon her longings for Trieste and had vetoed the Italian aspiration for Valona and an Albanian protectorate.

### III.  ITALY AND THE TRIPLE ALLIANCE

An ancient wrong, a contemporary grievance, and a clash of aspirations as to the future in the Adriatic and the Ægean, in Albania and Anatolia, thus divided Italy from Austria, while the two states were still allies. Because the bitterness was so great, Count Nigra had affirmed that Italy and Austria could only be open foes or actual allies and for thirty years Italian policy had deemed it wiser, since Italy was incapable of fighting Austria backed by German arms, to endure the humiliation incident to an alliance rather than to court the disaster which must accompany war.

Yet now, when one comes to examine the reasons for Italy's decision to join the foes of the Central Alliance, it is essential to grasp how completely this Triple Alliance had been for the Italians a marriage of convenience of a truly sordid character. From this alliance Italy could only derive security; for this security she paid the price which was passive adherence to conditions even then well-nigh intolerable and seemingly destined in the future to be fatal to all Italian aspirations. Italy desired to regain her "lost provinces" of Trieste and the Trentino; both were Austrian, and, while Austria showed no intention of parting with the Trentino, which gave her military control in a real sense of the Northern Italian Plain, which gave her the keys to the Valley of the Po and to the great industrial cities of the Savoy Monarchy, Germany and Austria both were necessarily and unequivocally determined to retain Trieste, Austria's sole considerable seaport and the prospective doorway of the Pan-German Mitteleuropa upon the Adriatic Sea.

The Libyan War of 1912 demonstrated unmistakably the futility of Italy's foreign policy. Austria had annexed Bosnia in 1908. France had acquired German consent to her supremacy in Morocco in 1909, after Agadir and in return for "compensations" paid to Germany in the Congo. Italy had long possessed the consent of France, Britain, and Russia to take Tripoli, but when she sought to realize her claim, at least as valid as that pressed by Germany for "compensations" when France took Morocco, the Italians found themselves confronted by the hostility of Germany and by the undisguised threats and menaces of Austria, while the Turkish resistance in Tripoli owed much to German inspiration.

And this Libyan War was, after all, the first clear expression of Young Italy. It was little understood outside of the Italian Kingdom. It was acquiesced in rather than encouraged in London, where many bitter criticisms were voiced by a press still Turcophile. It was accompanied by sharp clashes with France, whose Tunisian interests were affected and even injured. But the real opposition came from Italy's allies and every Italian step was greeted by protest and angry denunciation. Was it not Bernhardi who wrote in 1911 that wise German policy would have been served by German attack upon Italy and in behalf of Turkey at this juncture?

After the Libyan War the Triple Alliance, as far as Italy was concerned, was dead. When the World War broke, Italy hastened her proclamation of neutrality, thus giving France a real and incalculable advantage. After August, 1914, the single question became for the Italian people one as between neutrality and participation upon the Allied side. To join the Central Powers was almost inevitably to bring them the victory; but that victory meant the consolidation of German power from the Baltic to the Persian Gulf; it meant transforming the Balkans into a Hapsburg appendage; it meant that Austrian rule would descend the Adriatic to Valona; it meant that Greece, ruled by a sovereign who was a German Field Marshal and the brother-in-law of William II, would become a German puppet, and that Bulgaria, controlled by an Austrian Czarlet, would be but the corner stone in the arch that would bear German power from Europe to Asia.

To give of her blood and her treasure in such a cause could bring Italy no reward. There was no one of her ambitions which could be realized, nor was she prepared to listen to the German urgings to face westward and turn her attention to Tunis and to Algeria, to surrender her dreams of rescuing Italian populations along the Adriatic and seek to reclaim Corsica and Nice, which despite their older association with Italy were now contented and patriotic departments of the French Republic. Even if Italy cherished such aspirations, and she did not, German power could not protect her against British fleets, and her own cities and islands were bound to be victims of any such aggression against France, now allied with Britain.

### IV.   ITALY AND THE GRAND ALLIANCE

On the other hand, what would Italian neutrality achieve with respect to the Grand Alliance against Germany should it triumph?

Certainly it would earn temporary gratitude, a new friendship.  Neither the British nor the French would fail to recognize the service rendered even by neutrality.   But beyond this they might not go.   Russia was sponsor for the Serb dream of a new Jugo-Slavic state, including Serbs, Croats, and Slovenes, and on the maps of the Southern Slavs this state included Trieste as well as Cattaro, Fiume as well as Durazzo.

Nothing was more certain than that if the Grand Alliance won the war it would seek to limit and block German advance to the Balkans by the creation of a great Southern Slav confederation along the Adriatic, and such a confederation would have an area equal to that of continental Italy and at no distant date might become a rival on the Adriatic, possessing, as it would, all the good harbours and occupying those islands which are the naval keys to this inland sea.   As between the urgings of Russia, which had borne the burden of the battle, and the pleas of an Italy which had remained neutral, could any one doubt what view would prevail in London and in Paris, particularly as it was becoming a cardinal doctrine in Allied policy that a strong Slav state must be created to bar the road of Germany to the Golden Horn?

Nor was this all.   Italy looked both to Albania and to the mainland of Asia Minor for her future colonial expansion.   But when the Allied fleet approached the Dardanelles, Allied statesmen began to make bids for Greek aid, bids which were favourably heard by Venizelos, though ultimately repulsed by the Kaiser's faithful brother-in-law, the King of Greece.   Northern Epirus, the Greek cities of Asia Minor from Smyrna to the Adalian district, already marked by Italy for her own, were profered to the Greeks as the price for sending their army to Gallipoli.

Here again Italy was faced by an unmistakable fact.   Greece was her real rival in the Near East.   For five centuries the Greeks had cherished the dream of a restoration of the Byzantine Empire, a hope witnessed when their new King took the title of Constantine.   Given the Hellenic commercial ability, given the amazing vitality of the race and its capacity to endure and to reassert itself, nothing was more probable than that the Ægean would be turned into a Greek lake when Greece held both Salonica and Smyrna.   Nor was it less certain that this new, strong

state, by reason of its association with the Grand Alliance, would receive their guarantee after the war and would become their soldier in the
Ægean, as the new Slavic state would be their servant on the Danube
and along the Adriatic.

Thus neutrality was for Italy only less perilous than association
with the Triple Alliance. If she chose the German way, she sacrificed
to Germany and Austria directly all chance of realizing her dreams. If
she refrained from all part in the war she was faced with the probability
that a victorious Grand Alliance, able to speak with the assurance and
in the tone of the victor, would erect new states on the territory
which was claimed for Italy and that under the guarantee of the Grand
Alliance, these new Slavic and Hellenic states would shortly become
capable of defending themselves against all Italian attack, even if the
support of the Great Powers were presently withdrawn.

Policy thus fused with patriotic emotion in the Italian decision.
The memories of the old struggle for liberty and unity, which had failed
to complete the work of restoring Italy, since it left Trieste and the
Trentino outside the kingdom, shared in the Italian mind with patriotic
aspirations for the future, for the acquisition for Italy of a position
commensurate with her present power and worthy of the nation which
was the heir of Rome and the residuary legatee of Venice. From the
moment when the war broke the old memories and the old wrongs,
which had a present phase, made it imposible for the Italians to fight
alongside the Austrian and the German, but as Italy's past and present
demanded Austro-German defeat, her future required that she should
share in Allied victory that she might, once the victory was won, speak
as an ally in the congress in which peace terms would be made and claim
as one who had bore her share of the burden that portion of the profits
which Italian ambitions had already marked out.

It is necessary, at the outset of Italy's operations, to recognize the
distinction between her policy and that of the nations whose ally she
became. France fought for her life and, once Germany had forced a
new war upon her, for her lost provinces of Alsace and Lorraine. Britain fought for her imperial existence, tardily recognized as the ultimate

target of Germany. Russia had drawn her sword to save Serbia. The Turkish enlistment had raised the question of the Straits and the British and French had agreed to Russian possession at Constantinople. But, save in Turkey, Russian purposes were in the main those of liberation. She sought to free the remainder of Poland, still condemned to German and Austrian rule, to win liberty for the millions of Austrian and Hungarian Slavs, her race brothers, subjected to Teutonic and Magyar yokes.

But Italy, pursuing a policy which aimed at liberating the Italians of Trieste and the Trentino, not less clearly sought objects which were selfish and detrimental to the proper ambitions of the Greek and Serb races. She fixed her eyes upon lands which were peopled by races whose wish was not to be Italian but Hellenic or Slavic. And when the Russian Revolution was followed by a renunciation by the new Russian Government of all territorial ambitions cherished by the previous régime, certain of Italy's aspirations stood out in clear conflict with the spirit of her other Allies, who had adopted and in the main adhered to a programme which sought to liberate many races but to enslave none.

Italian purpose was thus, in a measure, tinged with a German spirit. Young Italy, like New Germany, like the Pan-Germans of Prussia, sought to serve the ends of the greater state they dreamed of, by the sacrifice of the nationalistic ideals of other races. Those who cried up Italy's claim to lands inhabited by race brothers along the Isonzo and the Adige cried down the claims of the Serb for Dalmatia and of the Greek for Northern Epirus and the islands of the Ægean which were far more Hellenic in character and more unitedly desirous of Greek citizenship than were the people of Istria Latin or clamorous for Italian sovereignty. It is necessary then to recognize that, great as was the military advantage incident to Italy's accession to the Allied cause, it necessitated certain compromises, which weakened the Allied cause on the moral side in the eyes of neutral mankind.

Nor is it less essential to recognize that when Italy entered the war her known purposes rallied the Southern Slavs to the House of Hapsburg and the troops which had fought indifferently against the Russian resisted with admirable tenacity and success each Italian assault along the

Isonzo. And in the same fashion, the Italian entrance gave new strength to Constantine in Athens and enabled him, with the support of many Greek patriots already enraged by Italian presence at Rhodes and in the Dodecanese, to prevent Venizelos from putting Greece into the war on the Allied side in the critical days of the following summer, when the fate of Serbia was at stake, as it earlier enabled him to veto the decision of Venizelos to send Greek troops to Gallipoli to aid the British army. Either step, had it been taken by the Greeks, might have changed the whole course of the war in the Balkans.

## V.  THE MARCH TO WAR

Having now set forth the reasons which made it always inevitable that Italy would one day take her place in the Allied ranks, the actual march of events can be reviewed with little delay. Italy's neutrality had been proclaimed on August 6, 1914. The pact of the Triple Alliance bound the high contracting parties to mutual defence, but the Italians asserted that it had no application in a war that was the result of an Austrian ultimatum designed to provoke war. Since the Italian course had been expected it created no surprise and little bitterness either in Vienna or Berlin.

In the days during which the German armies approached Paris, Italy was condemned to watch with ever-growing anxiety the prospective triumph of an ancient ally, whose course as a victor might be unfriendly toward the nation which had abandoned it at the moment of war. When the German advance was halted and thrown back, this anxiety disappeared. As the probability of a long war grew, it became more and more important that Italy should adopt a definite policy. In December, when Austria invaded Serbia and seemed destined to win a great victory, Italy called attention in Vienna to the provision of the Treaty of the Triple Alliance which asserted that if either Austria or Italy disturbed the *status quo* in the Balkans, the other should be entitled to ask compensation.

But the Austrian disaster at Valievo and the subsequent flight out of Serbia temporarily disposed of this question, although Italy, on Christmas Day, crossed the Straits of Otranto and landed troops at Valona in Albania, a step violently resented in Vienna. During the winter, while Russian armies continued to advance in Austria, Italian apprehensions were again aroused, this time by the fear lest Austria should collapse and a victorious Russia erect a Southern Slav Confederation along the Adriatic, including lands desired by Italy; and in the spring the sound of Allied guns at the Dardanelles stirred other anxieties not less keen. And all through this time the party which advocated intervention steadily grew stronger in Italy.

Germany sent her ablest diplomat, Prince von Bülow, allied to Italian nobility through his wife, to wage the battle against intervention. To his aid Bülow called all the vast financial agencies which Germany had established in Italy. He bought newspapers and politicians. He conducted a propaganda of colossal proportions. He became in fact almost a master of Italian affairs, and his success was in the end his ruin. The spectacle of a German controlling their public men, their press, and their policy eventually roused the Italians, and Bülow was presently greeted with the old Garibaldian hymn: "Stranger, begone out of Italy."

Again and again the Sonino-Salandra cabinet informed Vienna that Italian neutrality could not be maintained if Austria declined to make any concession in the matter of Trieste and the Trentino. Bülow himself undertook to persuade Austria to yield and ultimately Vienna grudgingly offered to cede a portion of the Trentino, including Trent, the delivery to be made at the close of the war as a reward for Italian neutrality.

To this Rome replied on April 8 by what amounted to an ultimatum, in which Italy demanded immediate possession of the Trentino, the separation of Trieste and its adjoining district from the Hapsburg Empire, and the cession of certain Adriatic islands. Trieste was to be constituted a neutral state between Italy and Austria.

To this Austria made no satisfactory response. Accordingly, on April 24, Italy at last made her arrangement with the Allies and on May 3 denounced the Triple Alliance. The end was now in sight.

At this moment Italy was seized by a patriotic emotion which can hardly be paralleled in history. The anniversary of the sailing of Garibaldi and his Thousand was at hand. D'Annunzio returned to Italy, the prophet and apostle of intervention. The country was filled with patriotic demonstrations, the cities were nightly the scenes of processions and of outbursts. More and more the spirit of the masses was becoming inflamed.

At this moment Bülow played his last card. Giolitti, the political master of the Italian Parliament, returned to Rome from seclusion. The man who had made and unmade cabinets, who possessed a political machine surpassing any similar American institution, journeyed to the capital for the purpose of overthrowing the Sonino-Salandra Cabinet, accepting new concessions from Austria, which Bülow had provided, and preserving Italian neutrality. Three quarters of the members of the Italian parliamentary body were his own. He controlled the prefects of the various provinces. He was backed by all the financial and industrial institutions which had German sympathies or were under German control.

What followed amounted to a bloodless revolution. The Sonino-Salandra Cabinet, conscious of Giolitti's strength and of his ability and purpose to upset and repudiate their agreement with the Allies made on April 24, resigned. Giolitti saw the King, but at this moment the Roman populace, fired by D'Annunzio's addresses, took charge. In a few hours the streets of the Eternal City were filled with thousands of citizens marching to the music of Garibaldi's hymn and boldly proclaiming that there would be war or revolution. The very safety of the House of Savoy was challenged when the masses came to believe that the King had joined Giolitti in his effort to avoid war.

In a few hours Giolitti was on his way back to the north, a political exile; the Sonino-Salandra Cabinet had been restored and the vote of confidence of Parliament had underwritten its agreement with the Allies. Italian policy had been dictated by "the Street," as Bülow now declared. On May 23 Italy was at war with Austria.

### VI. A GREAT VICTORY

The entrance of Italy into the war was a great victory for the Allies and almost a disaster for the Central Powers. Although Berlin and Vienna had long foreseen this eventuality, when it arrived its effect was not less considerable. It robbed the victory of the Dunajec of much of its meaning.   It inevitably postponed the arrival of a decision and thus diminished the chance of German victory.   It forecast the day when Italy would extend her declaration of war to include Germany and thus complete the forging of an iron circle about the Fatherland, as it now closed Italian ports to neutral ships which had hitherto brought copper and other materials necessary to German munition making. It gave to the war the character of the earlier Napoleonic struggles, when the whole continent rallied against France.

The Italian army, numbering more than 700,000 on a war footing and capable of almost indefinite expansion—given Italy's population of 35,000,000—had been reorganized since the outbreak of hostilities the previous year.   Lacking still in heavy guns and in the machinery of war—which democratic nations can purchase only after war has come and can be acquired in peace only by an autocratic state like Prussia, preparing for an attack upon its neighbours—it was still an accession of manifest importance; while the efficient and considerable Italian navy was able at once to take over a portion of the task of the French fleet, which had watched at the entrance to the Adriatic Sea.

On the other hand, the Allies naturally exaggerated the immediate effect of Italian intervention.   They did not rightly estimate the strength of the barrier fortresses which Austria had constructed nor accurately appraise the obstacles in the way of Italian progress.   Nor did they at first understand that Austria, long expecting the attack, had kept her troops on the Italian border on a war footing and was ready for the attack when it came.   Equally unknown to them was the fact that Austrian Slav troops would be rallied to the Hapsburg throne by the Italian attack and that out of these elements, next to worthless in the face of Russian troops, Austria would be able to fashion armies which, aided by heavy artillery, would check and subsequently defeat the Italians at the Isonzo and before Trieste.

These miscalculations led to grave disappointments and some unjust criticism as the war proceeded and Italy did not arrive at Trieste or Laibach.   Since Austria had made provision against the Italian assault before the Dunajec campaign was undertaken, when it came she did not have to recall troops immediately from the east. Italy's decision consequently failed to change the course of the Galician or Polish operations. Entering the war after the disaster of the Dunajec, Italy could not save Russia; and to expect this was unfair.

The failure of Italy to participate in the Gallipoli campaign and in the subsequent Balkan operation led to equally unjust criticism. Much of this was stilled when the Austrians made their great offensive through the Trentino the following spring and almost reached the Venetian plain. Then at last something of the Italian problem began to dawn upon the Allied publics. The Italian failure to declare war upon Germany gave just ground for complaint; the obvious clash between Italian and Serb ambitions and the coldness of Italian sentiment toward the Southern Slavs awakened resentment. Yet Italy not unnaturally reserved the right, having entered the war with fixed objects and with definite ends to attain, to pursue her course and serve her own interests first. In the end, this lack of mutual coöperation and of common purpose brought Italy to the edge of ruin in the closing weeks of 1917, but at the outset it merely checked the Allied enthusiasm at Italy's entrance into the war.

As for the Italian campaign of 1915, it was marked by no event of great importance. Along the Trentino and at the Isonzo, after brilliant initial advances, the Italian troops were brought up before the permanent lines of Austrian defence and thereafter made only inconsiderable progress. These operations and the whole field of Austro-Italian fighting will be discussed in the later phase, wherein real Italian progress begins, but in the period now under review Italy's service consisted in permanently fixing some hundreds of thousands of Austrian troops on the southwest, putting a new burden upon Austrian munitions and man-power and thus accelerating Austrian exhaustion. She was unable to do more, nor were France and Britain able to achieve much greater results in their 1915 offensive. And if the results of Italy's enlistment were thus disappointing, by her entrance a possible foe became for the Allies a help instead of a peril, and if the immediate value of the military aid was exaggerated the moral value could not be.

# CHAPTER EIGHT

## GALLIPOLI

### I
### ANOTHER SICILIAN VENTURE

Athens, facing a terrific struggle in the Greek peninsula, listened to the specious pleadings of Alcibiades and sent her best troops and her great fleet westward to Sicily to seek there a brilliant victory. The daring gamble failed, the army and ships were lost, and as a result Athens fell before Sparta. In the Gallipoli venture Britain was now to make, there was a fair parallel with the Athenian blunder and there was about Winston Churchill, who was responsible for the decision, much that would suggest Alcibiades.

To send old ships which, even if lost, would not change the naval situation was a legitimate gamble, given the profits that would accrue could the Straits be forced. But when the gamble turned out badly then was the point when British statesmanship and Allied strategy should have abandoned it. Yet the lure of Byzantium remained to tempt those who could not perceive that the war was to be won or lost upon the western front and that effective aid to Russia, now in danger, could come only along the front between the Channel and Switzerland.

Subsequent Parliamentary investigations have revealed the confusion and blindness which prevailed in British Cabinet circles when the Gallipoli campaign was adopted. Voices of warning were not lacking; naval and military authorities did not hesitate to remonstrate; but the words of the politician overbore those of the soldier. Sir John French, in the trenches, begging for men and munitions to hold a line still imperfectly manned, still lacking in guns and above all in high-explosive shells, could not make his appeals heard in the Cabinet Council. The stern warnings of Joffre were unheeded; even Kitchener succumbed to the civilian strategist. The result was one of the great blunders of military history, hardly equalled since that of Athens and destined to have evil consequences hardly less considerable.

The fallacy of the Gallipoli undertaking is patent. To defend a narrow peninsula, Turkey had not less than a quarter of a million veteran troops, armed, equipped, and officered by Germans. These troops were close to their base and could be munitioned and reinforced with little difficulty, while Allied troops had to be transported for more than a thousand miles by sea and their advanced bases in Egypt and Lemnos were separated from the field of operations by many miles of submarine-infested waters.

But the main obstacle lay in men and munitions. For this great undertaking Britain could not muster more than 120,000 men and the French wisely declined to send any but colonial troops, since they were still facing a foe on their own soil. Outnumbered two to one in any event, the British had no reserves at hand to supply the wastage, and such troops as would later become available would have to be diverted from the western front. There was no chance of a surprise, for the March effort to force the seaward gates of Constantinople and the delay following the defeat and withdrawal of the naval forces, had allowed more than a month for Turkish armies and German engineers to prepare for the next blow.

Looking backward it is easy to perceive that, had the troops squandered on Gallipoli been put in on the western front, the early British operations about La Bassée might have prospered and the autumn offensive at Loos might have resulted in the piercing of the German line and the consequent relief of Russian armies, by this time on the edge of ruin. The Gallipoli venture, first and last, used up not less than a quarter of a million of British troops and cost more than a hundred thousand casualties on the British side alone. For the Allies it became precisely what Spain was for Napoleon in his last years—an open sore, ever demanding more troops, ever eating up more of his resources in men and supplies, yet never offering any possibility of compensating advantages.

In Berlin the decision of the British to go to Gallipoli was hailed with the same enthusiasm which Napoleon had displayed toward similar ventures of the British in the early wars of his period, when British armies and fleets were scattered all over the world and thus removed from the decisive field, which was Europe. Germany had embarked upon a campaign to crush Russia. She had assigned to her armies in the west the defensive mission, which was comprehended in the task of holding their own front. She had stripped these armies of every division and gun that could be safely spared to give Mackensen his great force. That the British should send their troops away from this western front and thus make the task of the German defensive the easier was a piece of good luck hardly to have been expected.

## II.   POSSIBLE PROFIT

Those who defended the Gallipoli venture at the moment and subsequently, insisted that it had a fair chance of success and that this success, if attained, would have changed the whole course of the war. It was argued that Egypt could better be defended at Gallipoli than at Suez and that pressure upon the Turks at the Dardanelles would relieve the Russian armies on the Armenian front.   To open the Straits was to break down the blockade of Russia, to send munitions to her armies now collapsing for lack of them, and to restore Russian finance by enabling Russia to market her wheat in England and France and from the proceeds to pay her obligations.

But like many speculations, the alluring character of the prospectus was in direct proportion to the impossibility of attainment.   So far as one can judge there never was the slightest chance of success. Winston Churchill, on a celebrated occasion, asserted that the British were within a mile of supreme success, but the mile was the main Turkish position and this was as completely beyond their power to carry as the whirlpool and falls of Niagara are beyond the capacity of a sail boat to negotiate, although their extent is short and beyond lies the calm surface of Lake Ontario.

The brutal truth about Gallipoli is that it was a blunder of the first magnitude, which consumed more than a quarter of a million troops who

IN THE CARPATHIANS

An Austrian ski patrol cautiously advancing through a forest on the mountainside

## AUSTRIAN MACHINE GUNNERS SEEK A NEW POSITION

The men are on skis. The gun has been taken apart and roped to a sledge. The deep snow and steep slopes of the Carpathians rendered practically useless all troops not accustomed to these special conditions

## AUSTRIAN RIFLEMEN IN THE CARPATHIANS

Note the rests for the rifles and the skis. The third man is using a field-glass. Many of the private soldiers, even of the Austrian and German armies, were equipped with these, though the U. S. War Department found great difficulty in providing them even for officers, as most optical goods before the war were imported from Germany.

A HUNGARIAN CORPS IN THE CARPATHIANS RECEIVES INSTRUCTION IN THE ART OF
SKI-WALKING

A SKILFULLY CAMOUFLAGED MOUNTAIN SHELTER WHICH ACCOMMODATED
TWENTY-FIVE SOLDIERS

RUSSIAN ARTILLERY ADVANCING THROUGH A CARPATHIAN PASS

This was near the scene of Mackensen's great drive on the banks of the Dunajec. He followed the tactics previously used on a smaller scale by Sir John French in Flanders. Massing not less than 2,000 guns along a narrow front, he delivered a devastating fire and followed it up by "Mackensen's Phalanx," a mobile battering-ram composed of the pick of German first-line troops. Russia never recovered from the terrible blows of this battering-ram.

DISMOUNTED AUSTRIAN HUSSARS CHARGING THE RUSSIANS

The photographer secured this picture at the imminent risk of his life. One of the Austrians has already been hit by a Russian bullet. Lacking the bayonets customarily used in the charges of regular infantry these men are clubbing their rifles so as to be ready to "give them the butt" when they get to close quarters

AUSTRIAN TROOPS SILHOUETTED AGAINST THE HIGH SNOWS

IN THE HIGH PASSES OF THE CARPATHIANS

Austrian troops ready to oppose the Russian attempt to force the mountain barrier and penetrate the Hungarian plain. Heavy German reinforcements, countless German guns, and the most skilful German generals were needed to drive the Russians home. Unaided, the Austrians could scarcely have hoped to stem the Russian tide permanently—much less to thrust the Russians back in decisive defeat.

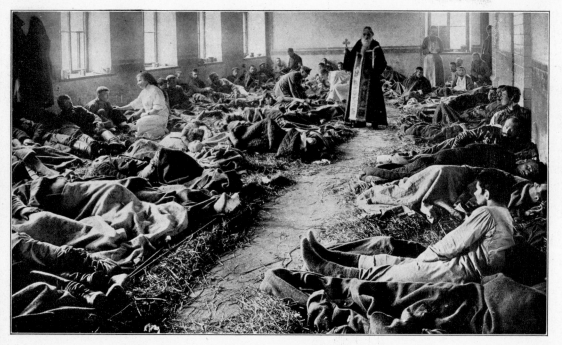

## HOLY RUSSIA—MORTALLY WOUNDED AT THE DUNAJEC

The upper picture shows defeated and wounded Russians trudging stolidly into the courtyard of a German hospital.

In the lower picture the interior of the hospital is seen, with the old priest of the Greek Catholic Church offering the consolations of religion to wounded and dying Russians as they lie on the straw-covered stone floor.

AUSTRIAN TROOPS ON A FORCED MARCH IN THE CARPATHIANS

might have been used effectively on the western front—conceivably so effectively as to rupture the German fronts; certainly with sufficient advantage to compel the Germans to relax their efforts in the east; unquestionably with enough of weight to have made impossible the German drive to the Golden Horn in the late autumn.

The German was the true enemy. When he was beaten the alliance of the Central Powers would collapse. To send a quarter of a million troops on a futile attack upon the Turk, doomed from the outset to defeat, was merely to lessen the pressure upon the German by just this amount. All summer long the British troops in Flanders lacked reserves, were starved as to munitions that the Gallipoli expedition might be supplied, yet such was the British shortage in men and munitions that the sacrifices in the west were futile and the Gallipoli army still lacked the necessary material for an equal fight with the Turk.

In the spring and summer of 1915 Britain lacked the resources to create and maintain an effective army on one front. Yet she undertook to maintain two great armies on two widely separated fronts. The result was failure in both fields. At Gallipoli some of her best officers and many of her best troops were sacrificed uselessly. On the west front the golden opportunity provided by the German decision to go east was permitted to escape, and in September the attack at Loos, which might have been a shining success, ended in a shambles, terminated in an appeal to the French by the British commander-in-chief to take over a portion of his lines, become too extended for his meagre force and his exiguous stock of ammunition.

Never in British history was there a more splendid example of the tenacity and the courage which have made the great empire. Nothing in English or world history surpasses the devotion of the men of Britain, of Australia, and of New Zealand, fighting under conditions beyond belief, enduring hardships beyond description, transforming what seemed an impossible operation into an undertaking that at moments seemed to promise victory, yet in the end failed as it was always doomed to fail.

The tragedy of Gallipoli is the hopelessness of it, the uselessness of the colossal sacrifice and the degree to which the valour and the unselfish devotion of officers and men were without gain to the cause for which they suffered.

On the other hand, it is impossible to escape the conviction that if the commander-in-chief, Sir Ian Hamilton, was charged with an impossible task, his conduct of the operations was open to deepest condemnation. The larger failure was probably not his, but his failure to make even a competent effort was glaringly displayed at Suvla Bay, where the only

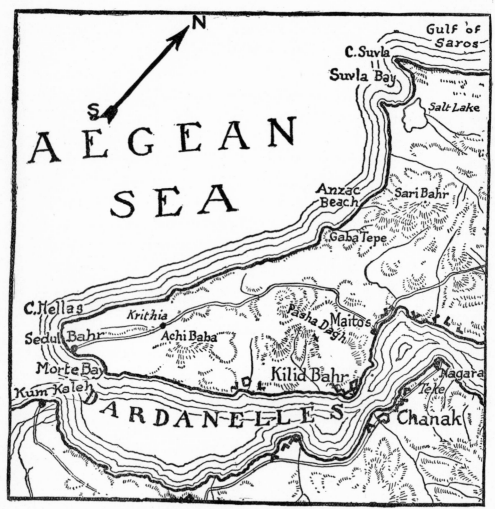

**THE GALLIPOLI PENINSULA**

The end of the Gallipoli Peninsula is shaped like a badly worn boot. The ankle is at Gaba Tepe, where the Australians landed; the heel at the Narrows, where were situated the forts commanding the Straits, which were the objective of the naval attack in March; whilst the toe is the promontory five miles wide, which ends at Sedd-el-Bahr. And it was at the toe that the main landing was made.

real chance of success—probably an apparent rather than a real chance —was lost under conditions that thoroughly warranted his subsequent removal. Nor is it possible to overlook the fact that the sufferings of the British army at Gallipoli were of the sort that had made the Crimean War an enduring reflection upon British organization and foresight. In this campaign the world was to see a British army hopelessly inferior to the Turk in all that makes the modern army effective and successful. Surely a more illuminating revelation could not be imagined.

### III.   GALLIPOLI

That portion of the Gallipoli Peninsula, which was the scene of the great struggle, has been aptly described by Sir Ian Hamilton as shaped like a badly worn boot. The ankle is at Gaba Tepe, where the Australians landed; the heel at the Narrows, where were situated the forts commanding the Straits, which were the objective of the naval attack in March; whilst the toe is the promontory, five miles wide, which ends at Sedd-el-Bahr. And it was at the toe that the main landing was made.

The three dominating hills of this end of the peninsula are Achi Baba, which, from a height of 600 feet, dominates the toe and blocks the road north from Sedd-el-Bahr; Sari Bahr which, at the height of 970 feet, overlooks the Anzac Cove and the Gaba Tepe position, the scene of the Australian operations; and the Kilid Bahr Plateau, directly above the forts at the Narrows and attaining a height of 700 feet. This latter was the main Turkish position and it was never reached by the Allied forces. An idea of the smallness of the distances may be gathered from the fact that at the ankle the peninsula is but five miles wide, while from Sedd-el-Bahr to the dominating positions at Kilid Bahr is not more than ten miles.

Apart from the beaches at the toe and another shallow beach under Gaba Tepe, the whole Ægean shore of the Gallipoli Peninsula is unsuitable for landing operations, since the hills rise abruptly from the sea. A third landing place, still farther to the north, at Suvla Bay, offered still greater advantages, which were seized upon in the final attack in August. But the relatively low foreshore of this bay is commanded by the Anafarta Hills, which were never cleared.   Actually, the British had three roads open to them for their advance—from Sedd-el-Bahr straight up the Peninsula to Kilid Bahr, a distance of ten miles; from Gaba Tepe eastward right across the peninsula, a distance of five miles; and from Suvla Bay first east and then south which was materially longer.   And from Sedd-el-Bahr they never were able to advance more than three miles.   From Gaba Tepe they got forward hardly more than one mile and the Suvla Bay effort ended in a complete fiasco, which doomed the whole enterprise.

The hills that rise abruptly from the shore slope downward and inward, giving the peninsula the appearance from the air of a spoon, hollowed out in the centre, and this made it next to impossible for the guns of the fleet to reach and destroy Turkish positions.   Moreover, the whole area was a series of confused gullies, steep hills, and deep ravines, covered with underbrush and admirably suited to the sort of fighting the Turk was best suited to offer.

The climatic conditions were indescribably bad.   In winter the peninsula was swept by the cold blasts from the Black Sea.   In summer it was baked by a tropical sun which dried up all watercourses and turned the country into a desert and a furnace.   All water for drinking had to be brought from Egypt or Lemnos.   At all times, all portions of the British position were within easy range of Turkish guns, the landing places were commanded by artillery, the expedition lived under shell fire.   There was no respite and no truce.

In the same fashion their rearward communications by sea were at the mercy of the weather.   All supplies, reinforcements, and artillery had to be landed under direct observation and fire.   No movement could be made without first advertising its character by the preparations carried out under the Turkish eyes.   A more hopeless, hapless position for a great army cannot be imagined, nor is there anything in military history since the Crimea to compare with the hardships of the men of Gallipoli.   The measure of this is found in the fact that while the battle casualties of the campaign were 112,000—25,000 killed, 75,000 wounded, and 12,000 missing—the hospital statistics revealed

96,000 admissions.   Thus the climate was almost as deadly a foe as the Turk.

No survey of the campaign would be complete without a mention of the admirable manner in which the Turk fought.   Standing on the peninsula by which, following the route of Xerxes, his ancestors had entered Europe five centuries before, he made a fight which commanded the unstinted praise of his British foe.   He not only fought well, but he fought cleanly.   In the intervals between desperate fighting the two armies observed those courtesies as to wounded which had been customary in other wars but had been banished on the western front by German savagery.   Not only did the Turks conquer their foe in the field, but they won his praise and his admiration for courage and for skill, for devotion and for military efficiency.

### IV.   THE BEGINNING

The naval attack on the Straits had failed on March 22.   It was more than a month later—on April 25—that the first landing party touched the Gallipoli shore.   The date is interesting.   On this day the Germans were making their desperate attack at Ypres and were on the point of launching their blow at the Dunajec.   Italy, on the preceding day, had made her agreement with the Allies, which was to bring her into the war in another month.   The campaign of 1915 was in full swing and the operation in the Near East divided world interest with the German bid for Ypres, still accepted as one more serious attempt to reach Calais.

Sir Ian Hamilton's force had been mobilized in Egypt and transported to Mudros Bay in the Island of Lemnos, which was to serve as its base.   He had with him three British corps, some 120,000 men, including the Australian and New Zealand corps, which, under the name of the "Anzacs" (Australian New Zealand Army Corps), was to win imperishable glory in defeat and demonstrate once more the solidarity of the British Empire, as the Canadians were proving it in Flanders and the South Africans along the Orange River.   To this force was joined a contingent of French soldiers, under General D'Amade, who had won reputation in the Shawia campaign in Morocco before the present war and rendered useful service to Sir John French in the retreat from Mons. D'Amade gave way shortly to Gouraud, one of the great French colonial figures, who lost an arm and had to leave in turn before long. The French contingent was a useful but not considerable help to the British. Its main contribution was through its artillery.

On the morning of April 25 the attack was made. The main British force was thrown against the Turkish positions commanding the beaches at Sedd-el-Bahr; the Australians were put ashore before Gaba Tepe; the French were sent across to the Asiatic shore to make a feint and attract Turkish attention. Actually they fought over ground that had seen the battle for Troy in the mighty Homeric drama.

The landing is one of the ghastliest of the incidents in the whole war. For a month the Turks had been preparing. Not only was the shore fortified, but the beaches, the shallows were covered by submerged barbed wires. Against this position the British were sent in open boats, partly but not effectively covered by the fire of the fleet. They made the landing, they made good their hold on the toe, but not less than 15,000 casualties was the price of the effort. As many troops were killed, wounded, or captured on this first day of the Gallipoli fighting as the United States sent to Cuba in the first Santiago expedition.

Afterward, in the next days, the effort to get forward was pressed. Under conditions beggaring description the remnants of the organizations that had made the landing sought to press on to Achi Baba, the first stage of the journey. They failed. When this first phase came to a halt through the exhaustion of the assailants, the Turks still held this height and the village of Krithia on its slopes. Actually the British army had inserted itself in a bottle, of which Achi Baba was the stopple. Before it now were positions impregnable, given its own resources. Some slight progress it was still to make on this front by a war of trenches, but in point of fact the road from Sedd-el-Bahr to the Kilid Bahr plateau, to the dominating positions above the Straits, was blocked.

As for the Australians, they had managed to get up the first slope of the hills above the Anzac Cove, where they had landed, but they were now condemned to hang on, their backs to the water, their trenches exposed to plunging fire, dominated by the Turkish positions on Sari Bahr. Their losses had been terrible, too. Gallipoli was now become a word of evil omen both in Australia and New Zealand. And despite new efforts and new devotion, despite still greater sacrifices, the Australians were not destined to make any further considerable progress eastward. Sari Bahr was to block them, as Achi Baba held up their comrades to the south.

In British strategy it had been planned that the Australians moving east, the British moving north, should converge in the centre of the peninsula and before the Kilid Bahr Plateau. The Turks had blocked both of the converging columns on their chosen positions and they were to hold them before these positions until the end of the campaign. And with this first desperate effort the original expedition came to the limit of its powers. It could do no more until it was reinforced, so great had been its losses. Henceforth Gallipoli was an open sore, daily wasting more and more of British vitality to no useful purpose.

### V. SUVLA—THE END

In May the difficulties of the Gallipoli army were enormously increased by the arrival of German submarines in Ægean waters. Hitherto the British fleet had been able to support the land forces while British submarines had made daring raids through the Strait and interfered with the seaward communications of the Turk. But on May 15 a German submarine was reported off Malta, while three days previously a Turkish torpedo boat, by a daring raid, had sunk the British battleship *Goliath* just inside the Strait, where it was coöperating with the French.

On May 26 a German submarine sank the battleship *Triumph*, which was covering the Australian position. The next day the *Majestic* met the same fate, and thereafter the fleet had to be withdrawn. The departure of the fleet, the withdrawal of its guns which were necessary to cover any real effort to advance and prepare the way for any attack which could hope for success, doomed the Gallipoli venture in the eyes of all military men who had not perceived from the outset that it was an impossible venture.

Yet the British would not give up the task. After long delays and many local engagements of only minor value they tried one more stroke. Meantime the cost in casualties was mounting rapidly. May had cost 38,000, including the casualties of the last days of April. Before July ended the toll was more than 50,000, while the French had also suffered heavy losses. In addition, the cost in sick was mounting in an alarming fashion. By August almost half of the men of the six original divisions had been killed, wounded, or captured, and fully a quarter more had been removed by illness. Not even in the terrible days of Ypres had the ratio of losses been greater than in some of the regiments of the 29th division at Gallipoli. But to reinforce the six original British divisions six more—three from the New Army, two territorial, and a mounted division from Egypt—had been sent out.

The final bid for success at Gallipoli was made in the first week of August and extended into the second. The main element in the strategy was the landing of a strong force at Suvla Bay, four miles north of the Australian position, and an advance by this newly landed force due eastward to the Anafarta range, which was the backbone of the peninsula and from which the British would command the Turkish lines of communication along the west side of the Dardanelles. At the same time the Australians were to make a frontal attack, the British before Krithia to push forward to hold the Turks before them. The Suvla Bay forces were to join hand with the Australians and the Turkish position would be enveloped, while the Australians, by their advances, would gain heights from which they could command the waters of the Strait.

The time was well selected. The Turks were celebrating the Ramadan and had no suspicion of the coming blow. The landing at Suvla was made without any difficulty and the Turkish surprise was complete. Meantime, the Australians had pushed out and seized the ground that was allotted to them to take. All now depended upon the energy and determination with which the Suvla advance was made. But here comes the first real collapse. Once the troops were landed they were permitted to halt. Hour after hour passed and no advance was made. The golden opportunity was slipping away as another brilliant chance had escaped at Neuve Chapelle, when the road to Lille lay open. August 7, the day of the Suvla landing, is the critical day on the Gallipoli front.

On August 8 there was a fair chance, but the Suvla force was still held back. The hold of the Australians upon the vital heights was becoming weak. The Turks were recovering and beginning their terrific counter attacks. August 9, with a faint hope left, Sir Ian Hamilton arrived and urged a night attack. His subordinates declared it was impossible. The commander-in-chief allowed himself to be overborne. Thereafter when the attack upon Anafarta was made, it was too late. Meantime the Australians had been pushed back off their extreme gains. The whole situation was as it had been. Forty thousand casualties in August had not changed the decision.

Whether the Suvla attack, had it been efficiently pushed, would have brought ultimate and complete victory may be doubted. The weight of judgment is against this belief, which long subsisted in the Gallipoli army itself. But no one could mistake that the failure doomed the whole campaign, as it quite justly brought the removal of Sir Ian Hamilton. After Suvla he still appealed for reinforcements. But all too late Britain called a halt. At last the truth was dawning, while, because of Russian defeat and Balkan complications, the necessity for some British offensive operation in the west, in conjunction with the French, to relieve pressure upon the Russians, was imperative.

From August onward Gallipoli diminishes in importance. By December, when the German successes in the Balkans had opened the road between Turkey and her great ally and made certain the arrival of German artillery at Gallipoli, evacuation was inevitable, and on December 19 the troops were withdrawn from Suvla. By December 20 the Anzacs were safely away. By January 9 the last troops had left the peninsula. No portion of the Gallipoli campaign was so successful as the evacuation, which cost neither men nor guns, although conducted under fire and within direct vision of the Turk.

The lesson of Gallipoli was to be emphasized at Kut-el-Amara, where another "side show" was to end in the surrender of a British army, rashly pushed forward on an impossible dash for Bagdad. The two disasters were to produce a profound impression in Britain and in the world they were to have a costly influence upon Balkan affairs. They were to contribute to raising German fortunes to unequalled heights. Taken in conjunction with the failure of the British at Loos— where 66,000 casualties was the price of a slight gain in ground and disorganization and inefficiency were revealed in staff administration comparable to the blunders and failures at Suvla—they were to lead to a total reorganization of British military machinery.

Had Sir John French been able to put to his work on the west front the quarter of a million troops wasted at Gallipoli, the results of the 1915 campaign might have been far different. Even a complete success at Gallipoli would not have saved Russia from her great disaster. It would not have weakened Germany, although it would have ended her dream of a Berlin-to-Bagdad empire. All too late the Allies were to realize that the war would be won or lost in the west. France was to pay at Verdun the price of British folly at Gallipoli, for because of Gallipoli losses Britain was still unready to move when the great German blow, the second assault upon France, came in February and March of the following year.

In sum, Gallipoli was for the Allies what Spain had been for Napoleon. It was in a measure what Syracuse had been for Athens. It was not a fatal blunder, since it did not immediately or eventually lose the war, but it did prolong it. It did accelerate the pace of French exhaustion and it did leave Germany free to strike at Russia and to strike so heavy a blow that Russia, after a temporary recovery, fell to revolution and disorder and in the summer of 1917 ceased to be of value as an ally. It was therefore the worst and most expensive defeat of the first three years on the Allied side—a defeat first correctly appraised when Serbia, threatened with ruin, uttered the despairing cry which could not be answered, because the men and the guns that might have saved the army, if not the nation, had disappeared in the Gallipoli gamble.

# CHAPTER NINE

## RUSSIAN COLLAPSE

### I
### AFTER LEMBERG

Lemberg fell on June 22. With the fall of the capital the Galician campaign loses its importance and becomes a secondary affair. In German strategy there were two clearly separated sections of the eastern campaign of 1915. The first was comprised in the clearing of Galicia of Russian armies; the second contemplated the reduction of the Polish salient, the capture of Warsaw and the various Russian frontier fortresses from Riga to Rovno. Yet always it is essential to remember that the geographical achievement was subordinated to the military. The main German purpose all through this campaign was to destroy Russian military power, either by a great and decisive victory—a Sedan many times greater than that which had destroyed the Third Empire along the Meuse—or by the cumulative effect of successive defeats.

By the first days of July the Russian situation was this: From the neighbourhood of Riga straight to the Niemen at Kovno the line ran north and south. From the Rumanian frontier northward to the Volhynian fortresses of Rovno, Dubno, and Lutsk the Russian front was also straight. But from Kovno on the north and Lutsk on the south the line turned westward, making a triangle with Warsaw as its apex. This was the great Polish salient of military parlance, a position so fraught with peril that long before the war Russian High Command had contemplated an evacuation of all this ground in case of a war with Austria and Germany and a stand behind the line of the Niemen, the Narew, the Bug, and great Pinsk or Pripet marshes.

The peril of the salient was just this: Austrian armies advancing from Galicia, German armies coming south from East Prussia, could they pierce the Russian lines, the sides of the triangle would meet behind Warsaw and would cut off the retreat of all the Russian armies within the triangle unless they had retreated in time.  The Russian position was the more dangerous because the two railroads vital to its defence, the Warsaw-Petrograd and the Warsaw-Kiev lines, were both but a short distance from the front, and a relatively insignificant advance, either out of East Prussia or out of Galicia, would enable the enemy to cut these. lines behind the Russian armies on the Warsaw front.

All the intricate and confused campaign between July and October in the east becomes easily comprehensible if one but glances at the map and identifies the chief characteristics of the Polish salient.   All German strategy is comprehended in the simple purpose to get behind the Russian armies in the Warsaw salient by breaking in the sides near the points where the triangle touches the main Russian line, from which it projects much after the nature of a cape.   This main purpose was not achieved, because each time the peril of envelopment became obvious the Russians promptly retired in the centre and held on to the sides of the triangle until the forces at the apex had retired.

The operation has three distinct phases.   In July the battle is for the Warsaw salient.   In August, after Warsaw has been evacuated, the Russian effort is to hold the base of the salient, the line from Riga southward through Kovno, Grodno, Brest-Litovsk and thence to the Volhynian fortresses.   This is prevented by German advances to the north and south, which threaten to put German armies behind the Russian centre at Brest-Litovsk, as they had menaced the old centre at Warsaw. Finally, in the third phase, the Russian armies become separated, gaps open between the various groups of Slav armies, and through these gaps the Germans penetrate.   Thus in September there is an hour of deadly peril for great Russian forces about Vilna.   They are actually enveloped for days, but they finally cut their way out and thereafter the eastern campaign gradually diminishes in importance and Russian and German lines begin to reëstablish themselves on the fronts they are to maintain for many months to come.

Of the German strategic purposes, that of clearing the Austrian territory was practically realized by July 1. The conquest of Poland, with the straightening of the eastern front and the capture of Warsaw, was realized on August 4, when Warsaw fell. The determination to expel Russia from all her frontier fortresses from Riga to Volhynia was realized, save in the important cases of Riga and Rovno, by the first days of September. No Russian army was captured or destroyed and to this extent the German strategy failed. Nor did the Germans quite reach that eastern front, easiest to hold and doubtless their ultimate geographic objective. Yet the result of their victories was the ultimate collapse of Russian military power.

## II. THE DOOM OF THE EMPIRE

In the period now to be examined we enter that doubtful and difficult region of Russian domestic politics. As the campaign closes the Czar, by a magnificent gesture, puts himself at the command of the beaten armies and under his leading they rally. Could his will have remained firm perhaps his empire might have been saved, but after a brave moment the Czar relapses into weakness, a pro-German and reactionary group seizes the reins of power, and Russian armies are betrayed to the enemy and the Russian Revolution made inevitable.

Already the disclosures that have been made possible by the Russian Revolution begin to reveal things long suspected. That the Russian generals and soldiers who fought so splendidly from the beginning of the war to the autumn of 1915 were betrayed by their government is no longer to be denied. That many of the German triumphs from Tannenberg to the end of the fatal campaign of 1915 were due to official betrayal of Russian interests is as plain now as it was a matter of conjecture two years before.

Time and again in the critical hours of the campaign of 1915 ammunition failed. The vital fortress of Kovno was surrendered to the Germans under conditions that were even in 1915 accepted as proof of treason. Hundreds of thousands of lives were sacrificed, great regions of Russia were devastated and lost to the enemy because of German intrigue in Petrograd and German influence amidst the reactionary elements of the Russian monarchy.    All this the Russian people knew. They learned in the summer of 1915 not merely to expect defeat in the war, but to hope for it as the first step in the destruction of the monarchy and the attainment of Russian liberty.

The campaign of 1915 destroyed the monarchy in the eyes of the people of Russia.    All the skill of the really great Russian generals— Brusiloff, Ivanoff, Russky, and Alexiev—all the devotion of the soldiers, all the unquestioned fidelity to the cause of Russia of the Grand Duke Nicholas himself were of no avail.    And when Nicholas disappeared into the Caucasus to win new but unavailing victories at Erzerum, the German influence about the Czar became dominant.    Thus, while at the moment the military aspect of the great Russian disaster claimed the attention of the world, it is probable that the generations that are to come will see the military events as significant merely because they were the prelude to the political changes, to the Russian Revolution, to all the great and terrible events of the winter and spring of 1917.

And on the larger side it is necessary to point out that, although at the moment Germany seemed to have failed in her chief purpose—to dispose of Russia as she had sought to dispose of France in the previous years—later events proved that Germany did reckon rightly and that when her armies had completed their great campaign in the east in the autumn of 1915, she had achieved the eventual ruin of Russia as a military factor in the war for the next two years at the very least.    For if the Russian armies were to win magnificent victories in the summer of 1916, the betrayal of Rumania by the Russian Government in the autumn was to destroy the fairest prospects the Allies were to have in the first three years of the war and thereafter the ruin was to be prompt and inevitable.

It is because it brought the Russian Revolution that the eastern campaign is chiefly significant.    It is because it was the first step in this ruin that the Battle of the Dunajec is bound to remain one of the memorable encounters of human history.    Looking now at the military operations of the period, we must see in each episode the meaning in Russian political history quite as clearly as in the military history of the war. Revolution is marching side by side with Mackensen and Hindenburg in all this period and because it was bound to disorganize and well-nigh destroy Russian military efficiency, and Russia's value as an ally of the western powers, we must see Revolution as an ally of the Germans.

When they had reached the threshold of winter the Germans could afford to halt. The example of Napoleon forbade another adventure with Russian winter on the road to Moscow. Thenceforth they could wait until Revolution, entering through the breach they had battered in the walls of the Romanoff imperial structure, should complete that destruction of Russian military strength which they had begun at the Dunajec and carried to the Dwina.

### III. WARSAW

In the first days of July the situation on the eastern front was this: A German army, which had been landed at Libau, was moving east and north on the front between Dvinsk and Riga, with these two towns as objectives. To the south from the Niemen west of Kovno to the Vistula below Warsaw a group of German armies under Hindenburg was preparing to thrust south through the Niemen-Narew-Bobr line of fortresses covering the Petrograd-Warsaw railroad. A second group of armies, under Prince Leopold of Bavaria, faced Warsaw and Ivangorod along the Bzura-Rawka line, which had been unchanged for many months. South of the Upper Vistula a third army group, commanded by Mackensen, was beginning a thrust northward across the Warsaw-Kiev railroad.

It was plain at the outset that if either of the two flank operations succeeded the Warsaw salient must go. The mission of Leopold was merely to continue pressure upon the apex of the triangle and snatch any profit from a Russian disaster on another field. These three German army groups were faced by three Russian groups commanded by Alexiev, Evarts, and Ivanoff. There were as many as a dozen German and Austrian armies on this front, while the Russians were less numerous both in armies and men. Always the Germans possessed an enormous advantage in munitionment and in heavy artillery, while Russian munitions were to fail at many critical moments in the next weeks.

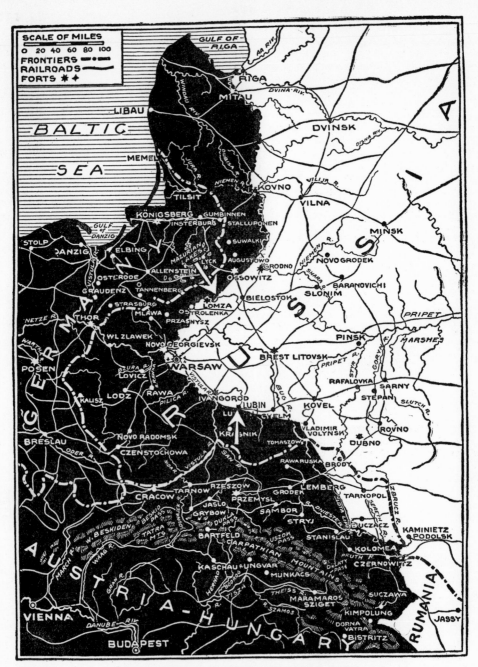

THE WARSAW SALIENT IN JULY, 1915

The *white arrows* show the lines of advance of the Germans under Mackensen and Hindenburg.
Compare this map with the one on page 193, showing the similar manœuvre of the Allies on the
western front.

THE FALL OF WARSAW, AUGUST, 1915

The Russian rear-guard surrenders to the Germans, and the Russian main body sullenly withdraws from the city

THE FALL OF WARSAW—AUGUST, 1915

The triumphant entry of Prince Leopold of Bavaria, and the looting which often follows a German success

About July 5 opening engagements of the first phase of the new campaign begin. The Archduke Joseph and Mackensen are pushing north. They have passed the Russian frontier and are moving upon Lublin and Cholm on the Warsaw-Kiev railroad. They are beginning to be handicapped now by the fact that they have entered a region of poor roads and are beyond the Galician network of railroads. The Russians, on the contrary, are now near their own rail lines and bases. And on July 9 the Archduke, having pushed forward too rashly and thus gotten out of supporting distance of Mackensen, is suddenly attacked and smartly beaten by Evarts at Krasnik, south of Lublin, losing many guns, flags, and some thousands of prisoners.

Mackensen now comes to the aid of his ally, but there is a marked slowing down of the German operation on this side of the Polish salient. In the third week of July there is still a remote basis for hope that the Lublin-Cholm position can be held.

But on July 25 one of Hindenburg's armies, commanded by Gallwitz, suddenly strikes north of the salient and along the Narew, aiming to reach the Petrograd-Warsaw railroad behind Warsaw. After desperate fighting Gallwitz gets across the Narew on July 25. But he, in turn, is forced to slow down. Yet on this same day Mackensen is again getting forward and is within ten miles of Lublin. Both sides of the salient are now in grave danger. To add to the peril, one of Leopold's armies has crossed the Vistula between Ivangorod and Warsaw, finding a weak spot resulting from the transfer of troops to meet Mackensen's thrust.

Warsaw is now doomed. Indeed a decision to evacuate had been taken as early as July 15, although there were moments subsequently when it seemed possible that the Russians might hold on. Lublin falls on July 30. The Warsaw-Kiev line, one of the vital railroads of the salient, is now cut. Therefore, on August 4, the Russians clear Warsaw and Prince Leopold's army enters the Polish capital one year to a day after the British declaration of war transformed the character of the contest into a world struggle. The Battle of the Dunajec had been won on May Day; less than a hundred days later the Germans were in Warsaw.

With the fall of Warsaw the next problem posed is whether the Russian armies can escape—will they be able to get east of the breaches in the sides of the salient before the armies of Mackensen and Hindenburg reach their lines of communication?

Again, as at Mukden, the Russians displayed their great capacity for successful retirement. By August 15 there is no longer any danger of an immediate envelopment, the Warsaw apex of the salient has been safely cleared, the road to Brest-Litovsk lies open, and the barrier fortresses along the Niemen-Bobr-Narew have fulfilled their final mission—those of the Narew are now doomed and there is no great purpose in holding them too long. Far to the south, too, the advance of Mackensen, aimed at Brest-Litovsk, has failed to move at a rate which would threaten envelopment. The first stage of the retreat is safely passed.

### IV.  KOVNO, BREST, VILNA

For the Russians the next problem is their ultimate rallying point. Like Joffre after his early defeats, the Grand Duke Nicholas has now to select a point at which to stand and counter-attack, having made his reorganizations. The line is fairly obvious. From Riga to Kovno the Russians are still holding off Below's army, striking east from Libau. From Kovno, which is a fortress of real strength, southward the east bank of the Niemen offers a safe position as far as the fortress of Grodno. Brest-Litovsk is an entrenched camp offering a good base for the Russian centre. To the south the Volhynian fortresses of Rovno, Lutsk, and Dubno hold.

We may assume that the Grand Duke hoped to make his stand on this line, which had been selected long before the war as the first line of Russian defence in a war with Austria and Germany. But on August 17 Kovno suddenly surrenders under circumstances which suggest treachery and later bring the commander to trial for alleged betrayal of his country. Kovno gone, the hope of holding the Niemen-Bug line is at an end and the flank armies on the north are in grave peril, which will culminate in the critical days about Vilna. Two days later the great fortress of Novogeorgievsk, below Warsaw, falls. Its capture was always inevitable; its mission was identical with that of Maubeuge in the great Anglo-French retreat of the preceding year. It commanded the Vistula, the best line of transport for the Germans, and covered the railroad line coming south out of East Prussia by Mlawa. A large garrison and many guns were taken, but although the defence proved to be shorter than was expected, there was no suggestion of such treachery as had cost the Russians Kovno. Nor did its fall have any effect upon the operations to the eastward save as it opened new lines of communication for the Germans.

Meantime away to the north a joint naval and military descent upon Riga with an attempted landing at Pernau is blocked. In the same fashion the Russians, falling back behind the Dwina from the Gulf of Riga to Dvinsk, hold up a dangerous drive of one of Hindenburg's armies for the extreme northern flank of the Russian line. But on the south Grodno falls on September 4, while Brest-Litovsk has to be abandoned a week earlier, on August 25. And at the precise moment Grodno is lost to the north, Lutsk and Dubno, two of the three Volhynian fortresses, fall. All chance of a stand on the Niemen-Bug line has now disappeared and the Germans are across both rivers, still aiming at the rear of the Russian armies.

Now, on September 5, the Czar takes command of his armies. The Russian Cabinet through Sazonov issues a solemn declaration that Russia will make no separate peace, thus answering German reports. And at this moment the campaign enters its critical stage. The Russian armies are now scattered and that between the Niemen and the Bug is in deadly peril. The disaster of Kovno on August 17 has its sequel about Vilna on September 20, when a great Russian army is enveloped on three sides while large contingents of German cavalry cross its only line of retreat. Berlin begins to hint at a Sedan and the world awaits with tense interest the final act.

Once again, as at Lodz, the Russian escapes. The stolid infantry smash their way through the German cavalry obstacle. By September 21 the road to Minsk is clear—the last Russian army has escaped all real peril of destruction. Far to the south Brusiloff is making a counter-

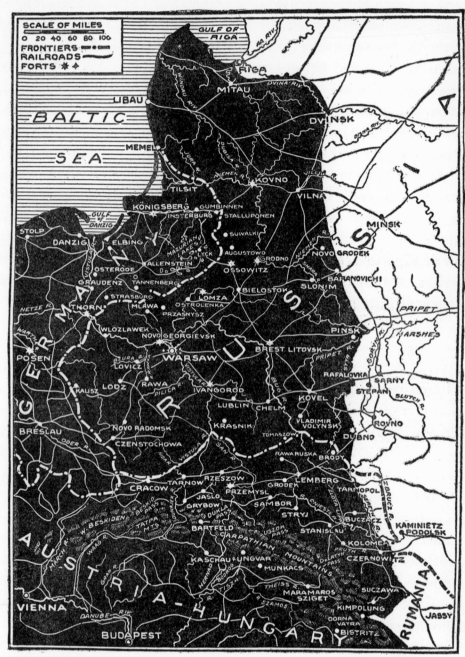

WHERE THE RUSSIAN RETREAT ENDED IN SEPTEMBER, 1915

offensive which temporarily retakes Dubno and Lutsk and assures the Russians of a permanent hold upon Rovno. Already winter is at hand and the German campaign is visibly slackening.

October 1 the end has in fact come, although there will be struggles about Riga, which will be successfully defended for two years more, and, all along the front, minor contests for certain local positions which have a value in establishing the permanent lines of the two armies, since they are now to return to a war of position, to trench warfare after five months of fighting in the open—five months of a war of movement which in numbers engaged, in prisoners captured, in territory conquered, can only be compared with those great campaigns of Napoleon in his younger days. And even the Napoleonic triumphs will unquestionably seem small when a later generation comes to compare the results of Marengo, Austerlitz, and Jena with the German achievement between the opening battle of the Dunajec and the closing drama at Vilna.

## V. AFTERMATH

While Berlin and Vienna celebrated the great successes, London, Paris, and Petrograd rejoiced over a German failure to destroy Russian military organization, capture Russian armies, or get Riga. Allied critics expatiated upon the weakness of German strategy as proved by the escape of Russian armies. Yet the fact seems to be that the German method made the prospect of great captures quite unlikely. Napoleon had said that he won his great victories by the legs of his soldiers. German victories had been won by their artillery.

Such an enormous machine as the Mackensen "phalanx" could only move slowly at best over favourable ground and with good lines of communication behind it. As the German advance when it reached Russian territory had to move over country devastated by retreating armies, employing ruined roads and hastily repaired railroads, its speed was necessarily slight. And when the German and Austrian armies undertook to act without the aid of the heavy guns, they incurred heavy losses and the Austrians frequently suffered real defeats. In the Marne campaign the Germans had outrun most of their ammunition and many

of their heavy guns.   This had been an important factor in the ultimate
loss of the great battle.

In Russia, a year later, the same mistake was not repeated.   The guns
were brought up; breaches were beaten in the Russian lines; the infantry entered the breaches, thus threatening a section of the Russian front
with envelopment and their troops in this section retreated to a new line.
Then the process was repeated.   As long as the Germans had to face
troops without heavy guns there was but one possible ending to such
struggles.   The Russian defeats, the destruction of Serbia, the terrible
disaster of Rumania a year later, these were all the direct result of the
German tactics based upon the German supremacy in artillery.

When the same tactics were employed against the French at Verdun
they failed because the French were able to bring up heavy artillery.   In
the same way the Germans at the Somme, themselves faced by a great
concentration of heavy artillery, were able to prevent disaster, although
the superiority of Anglo-French artillery compelled gradual retirement
and the Somme, on a reduced scale, is a repetition of the great Russian
campaign of 1915, with the Germans playing the losing part.

The last days of September mark the real termination of the great
eastern campaign, and the end was in small part at least influenced by the
tardy but terrific effort of the British and French in the west to relieve
the pressure upon their ally.   Largely because of this effort the Germans
failed to get what must be regarded as their extreme geographical objective—that lateral railroad which descends from Riga to Rovno and
would have made an ideal line of communication between the German
armies could they have pushed beyond it along the whole front.   In the
same way they would have profited had they been able to take Riga,
which would have been even more useful than Libau as base with the
coming of spring.   But it was the Russian navy which saved Riga.

Had the British and French been able to make a real offensive in the
spring, the German offensive might not have broken in the Polish salient
and conquered Poland.   An offensive in the summer might have exposed
German armies to deadly peril east and west, because while the masses
of the eastern armies were committed to a great and difficult operation in

a country devastated by the retreating Russians, they would not have been able to detach any considerable reinforcements, and such reserves as they could send west would have been long in arriving.

But France tried in Artois and failed to achieve any great result. Britain, her new troops in large measure drawn off for Gallipoli, was incapable of any considerable effort whatever. Conceivably the fate of Warsaw was sealed by the Dardanelles venture. Certainly the great and permanent Russian disaster would have been avoided had the British been able to make a real effort between April and the last days of September. And it is small wonder that all through this terrible summer the Russians watched with ever-growing apprehension Allied failure to move in the west; that Warsaw and Petrograd alike cried out for help vainly in July and August.

In her East Prussian campaign in August and the first days of September, 1914, Russia had suffered terrible disaster, but the effect of her rash drive had been to draw off German troops intended for the French field operations, even if, as is now held to be the case, no German corps were actually transferred from the west to the east before the Marne. But what Russia had done for her Allies they could not do for her and thus the Grand Duke failed where Joffre had succeeded. He saved his armies, but more he could not do.

# CHAPTER TEN

## THE BATTLES OF YPRES

### I

### THE BATTLEFIELD

The first campaign in the west ended with the final repulse of the Germans before Ypres in November, 1914. But the Russian campaign in the east proceeded without interruption from the opening operations of August, 1914, until the final halt of the Russian retreat far within Russian territory in September and October of the following year. Actually this campaign changed character when the German victory at the Dunajec finally deprived the Russians of the offensive and ended the endeavour of the Russian armies to dispose of Austria. Thus the real conclusion of the first campaign of the war seem to me to be at the Dunajec and not at the close of the First Battle Ypres.

In the volume describing the first phase, therefore, I briefly referred to the Second Battle of Ypres, which began before the Dunajec but lasted beyond the period of this great conflict in the east, thus preserving the temporal relation between the eastern and western campaigns. Yet actually the Second Battle of Ypres belongs to the campaign of 1915 in the west, it had consequences fatal to the Allied plans for their spring offensive, and it caused a disorder in Allied strategy which endured for many months. For these reasons and because in addition the Ypres battlefield became in the fourth campaign—that of the summer and fall of 1917—the scene of the principal Allied offensive of the year, and as the First Battle of Ypres was the most considerable British battle in all the history of the race up to the end of 1914, there is, perhaps, warrant for reviewing at this time the operations in the area that became forever memorable as the "Ypres Salient," and for studying the ground and restating the relation of the Second Battle of Ypres to the whole western campaign of 1915.

Turning first to the examination of the country itself, it should be remembered at the outset that Ypres is in the midst of the typical Flanders region—flat country marked by innumerable little brooks and rivulets, many of them canalized for centuries. This country begins as far south as Bethune and stretches north to the estuary of the Scheldt. Hills, mentioned so frequently in the battle despatches, are in reality but gently sloping elevations. Just as the American who is familiar with the history of the Battle of Waterloo and has read of the height of Mont St. Jean stands in amazement looking out upon the field itself when he first sees it and recalls, not the rugged country of the Appalachian seaboard but the prairies of the West, so he would view the district between the Lys and the Yser, on which was fought a battle greater than Waterloo and only less momentous in human history, for, had the Germans broken through to Calais, they might conceivably have abolished most of the consequences of the French victory between Paris and Verdun.

Bearing in mind, however, this qualification as to the stature of the hills about Ypres, it is still necessary to recognize that they played a decisive part in the various contests and that for the possession of the most considerable of them three battles were fought—one in October and November, 1914, a second in April and May, 1915, and the third and greatest, in the size of the armies engaged, from June to the end of the campaign of 1917.

To start at the beginning, there is between Bixschoote, at the edge of the marshes along the Yser River, and Warneton on the Lys, a fifteen-mile stretch of solid ground, that is, ground suitable for the movement of guns, transport, and large bodies of men. West of Bixschoote is the marshy region which was flooded when the Belgians closed the sluices at Nieuport in the critical days of the Battle of the Yser. South and east of Warneton, that is, on the right bank of the Lys, Allied operations were rendered impossible by the German occupation of Lille, with its forts and defences, which were, despite their contemporary condition, too great an obstacle for Allied resources either in 1914 or 1915.

The solid ground between the Lys and the Yser was then in the nature of a sally-port, should an army come north and seek to advance down the Lys valley toward Ghent and Bruges. On the other hand, for an army moving south it was the main gate to Calais and Boulogne, to the Channel ports facing the English coast, once the Yser front had been closed by inundation and the front south of the Yser barred by adequate armies. Could an army moving north push up to Roulers and Menin it would insert a wedge between hostile armies operating on the coast in front of the Yser and those to the eastward about Lille. Could an army moving south thrust through this gateway it would similarly intervene between the army defending the Yser front and the other forces before Lille. And when the British army moved north in October, 1914, its main purpose was to isolate the Germans advancing along the coast from those about Lille, while the German purpose, when the offensive passed to them, was to push down to Calais, isolating all the troops west of Ypres, the Belgian army, and a French force sent to aid the Belgians.

## II.  THE MESSINES-ZONNEBEKE RIDGE

Ypres, itself, lies in a little basin, about the tiny Yperlee stream which flows west to the Yser. It is the junction of several roads and railways and through it passes a canal from the Lys to the Yser. It was a fortress in the Eighteenth Century and some of the ramparts of Vauban have survived the artillery of Krupp, but these had no value on the contemporary military side. Of the roads and railroads the more important from west to east were: the Bethune-Bruges railway, which came up from the south and, after leaving Ypres, crossed the canal near Boesinghe, passed through Langemarck, and continued thence to Thourout; the Ypres-Roulers railway and highway, which paralleled each other and ran northeastward to Roulers; and the Menin Road, which ran straight from Ypres southeast to Menin on the Lys. A mile south of this last was the canal connecting the Lys with the Yser and Ypres with Commines.

South, east, and northeast of Ypres, at a distance of rather less than three miles, is the famous Messines-Zonnebeke Ridge, which is the most important geographical detail in the entire country. This ridge runs from southwest to northeast. It is at no point more than two miles wide and at many not more than one. Its highest point is at the south

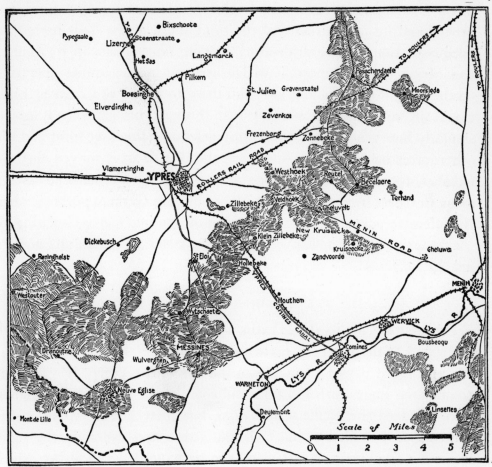

THE ENVIRONS OF YPRES AND THE MESSINES-ZONNEBEKE RIDGE

near Messines, where it is 250 feet above the level of the sea; at the other end, beyond Zonnebeke, it is rather less than two hundred feet. At no point is it more than a hundred feet above the surrounding country and it rises in gentle slopes, making a far more impressive showing on the map than upon the vision of the tourist.

Along this ridge, from south to north, are a number of small villages, forever famous in British battle history. These are: Messines,

Wytschaete, Hollebeke, Klein Zillebeke, Zandvorde, Gheluvelt, and Zonnebeke. North of the last it narrows to a point at Paschendaele. Actually this ridge is the watershed between the Lys and the Yser. Down its gently sloping western flanks flow a number of brooks which reach the Yser west of the inundated district. Eastward, over a much shorter course, flow other brooks leading to the Lys. Save in rainy weather—unhappily frequent in this weather-cursed corner of Europe —these streams are not obstacles to military operations.

Separating the streams which flow west to the Yser are a number of lower ridges running at right angles to the main Messines-Zonnebeke Ridge, the only one of importance in the present narrative being that north of Zonnebeke, which first borrows the name of Grafenstafel and then of Pilkem. It is the natural extension of the front of an army standing on the main ridge and troops in position on this Pilkem-Grafenstafel elevation would cover the flank of an army on the main ridge. On the other hand, were both the southern end of the Messines-Zonnebeke Ridge and the western end of the Pilkem Ridge in the possession of an enemy, the position of an army defending Ypres would be exceedingly dangerous because its rear and communications would be under the fire and observation of its foe. And it is worth recalling that the Messines position was lost in 1914, the Pilkem in 1915.

So much for the general topography of the country. Bear in mind again that an army holding all the Messines-Zonnebeke Ridge would look down on a vast sweep of country to the east and southeast. It would be able through its observation balloons to see as far as Lille, to sweep the whole of the upper valley of the Lys. Its heavy artillery in position behind the ridge would be able to command the Menin-Roulers road five miles to the east and play havoc with enemy communications, while its operations would remain hidden to the enemy, save for aërial observation, and its communications would be beyond reach of effective bombardment. Once, however, should the army be driven over and off the ridge, it would lose all these advantages and would be huddled in the Ypres basin, in a position which it would cost a steady and terrible wastage to hold and would always be a danger point.

It is worth recalling, too, that the Battle of Ypres, the first and in many ways the most famous encounter, was accidental, like Gettysburg. Neither army expected to encounter the other on the ground on which the meeting actually took place. And it is equally interesting to recall that the First Battle of Ypres was the last battle of the old-fashioned sort, that is, a battle in the open as contrasted with trench warfare, a conflict in a war of movement rather than in positional warfare on the western front up to the moment these lines are written in October, 1917, after the third anniversary of the opening contests about Ypres.

### III. THE FIRST BATTLE OF YPRES

On October 14, 1914, the first British troops reached Ypres. They comprised the immortal Seventh Division, commanded by General Rawlinson, which had landed at Ostend a few days before and had covered the retreat of the Belgian army, aided by some French formations. At this moment the Belgians, closely followed by General von Besseler's army, which had taken Antwerp and was advancing along the coast roads, were already near the Yser line, which they were to hold, and French troops were being railed up from the south to support them. Bad as was the condition of the Belgian army, it was still believed—justly as the result proved—that it would be able to hold the Yser line.

At this moment Allied High Command believed that between the German army approaching the Yser and the northern end of the main German front, which now extended from Switzerland to Lille, there was a wide gap, squarely in front of Ypres and extending from Menin to Roulers. Field Marshal Sir John French had sent Sir Douglas Haig north with the First Army Corps; Allenby's cavalry already about Armentièrres was to coöperate with it; and this force, together with the Seventh Division, seizing the crossings of the Lys from Menin to Courtrai, was designed to turn the extreme flank of all the German armies, aim at their communications, and compel a retirement from the coast toward Brussels, which was not felt to be beyond the reach of the Allies. Such a success would isolate Besseler on the Yser and probably lead to the capture of his army. In any event, it would release Lille and the industrial regions of northern France, now firmly held by the German armies which had been brought north and west from the Aisne and Lorraine fronts. And in conformity with this strategy, French ordered Rawlinson to move out of Ypres on October 17 and seize the crossings of the Lys at Menin.

Once more, as at Mons, British information was wholly out of accord with the facts. Actually the Allies had, in or approaching the region between the Lys and the Yser, less than 100,000 men, of whom only some French cavalry and Rawlinson's Seventh Division had actually arrived, while the Germans were moving four corps and some other formations, upward of half a million men, into this Ypres sector. Already aware of an impending change, but still unable to measure the extent of the threat, Rawlinson conformed to the imperious order of French and the next day moved the Seventh Division out to Zonnebeke.

On October 19 the Seventh Division sent out a brigade from Zonnebeke which actually reached the Roulers-Menin highroad, but there it encountered the advance guards of two German corps and was compelled to fall back rapidly to Zonnebeke. October 19 thus marks the end of the advance toward Menin and the crossings of the Lys. That night Sir Douglas Haig reached Ypres and the next day his First Army Corps came up. At once there was posed the question as to whether it should be put in to the east to support the Seventh Division on the Messines-Zonnebeke Ridge north of the Menin Road, or sent north to cover the flank from Zonnebeke through Langemarck to Bixschoote. Unless it was sent to the support of the Seventh Division there was now danger that Rawlinson would be overwhelmed, but if it was sent thither, then a gap would open in the Allied line between Zonnebeke and the marshes, and the Germans coming south through Langemarck would outflank both the British and the Belgians, drive a wedge between them, and have an open road to Calais and Boulogne.

Sir John French chose to risk the former peril and sent Haig north. When he was in position the Allied line from Switzerland to the sea was complete, but from the Lys to the Yser it was incredibly thin and for some days no reinforcements were available, as the French troops Joffre was sending up could not arrive before the 23d and did not all come until the 24th. As the First Battle of Ypres began, then, the British held the front from the inundated district at Bixschoote along the Pilkem and Grafenstafel ridges to the Messines-Zonnebeke Ridge east of this town, and thence south along the ridge through Becelaere and Zandevorde to the Commines Canal. South of the canal Allenby's cavalry held the Messines-Wytschaete sector with ridiculously insignificant cavalry screens. October 20 the real battle opens.

From October 20 to October 31 the fighting about Ypres was intense. On October 23 and 24 the arrival of the French Ninth Corps allowed Sir Douglas Haig to bring his First Corps from the Pilkem-Grafenstafel to the Messines-Zonnebeke Ridge and thus reinforce the Seventh Division, which was rapidly approaching the point of annihilation. But despite all effort the British were slowly but surely driven from the crest of the Messines-Zonnebeke Ridge and on October 31 their line was actually broken on the Menin Road, near Gheluvelt. This was the crisis of the whole battle, the moment when Sir John French himself sent the cooks, the hostlers, and every available man to the front line.

A lost battle was saved by the sudden appearance of the 2d Worcesters on the flank of the Germans advancing on the Menin Road west of Gheluvelt. The line was restored, but Gheluvelt was lost, as Zanvorde had been, and the front now ran from Zonnebeke south through the Polygon Woods to a point on the Menin Road just west of Gheluvelt. Like Meade after the first day of Gettysburg, French had been battered into a new but strongly defensible position; from Zonnebeke to the Menin Road the new front was now to endure for many months and never to be lost to a direct attack. But it was an exhausted and almost annihilated force which now held the line.

On November 1 the Germans shifted their attack to the Messines-Wytschaete front and seized the southern end of the Messines-Wytschaete Ridge. This was their greatest success in the whole battle and a French army corps which arrived the next day and retook both

Messines and Wytschaete was unable to hold either.  The capture of Messines and Wytschaete really created the Ypres salient.  Henceforth the Germans, from the highest ground in the whole region, looked down upon the rear and commanded the communications of the British in and east of Ypres.  After November 1, the Battle of Ypres continued

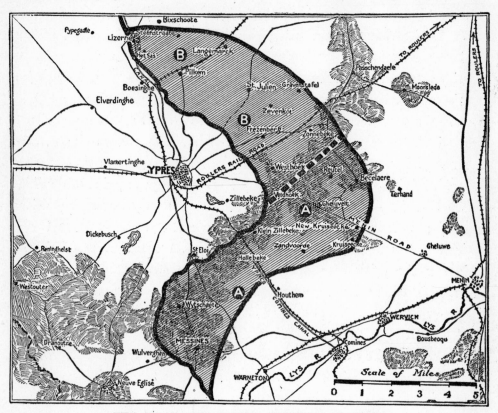

**THE FIRST AND SECOND BATTLES OF YPRES**

*A-A* shows the ground lost to the Germans in the First Battle, October 20 to November 11, 1914.
*B-B* shows the additional territory lost in the Second Battle, April 22 to May 8, 1915.
In the First Battle the Germans won the hills of Wytschaete and Messines; in the Second they took the Pilkem Ridge on the other side of the salient.  They held on here till the summer of 1917, when British advances abolished the whole salient.

with diminishing energy up to November 11, when the Prussian Guard made its celebrated attack, temporarily pierced the British line between Gheluvelt and Veldthook on the Menin Road and was thereafter annihilated.

The eleven days between October 21 and November 1 were the days of the great stress on the British front, and in this time that portion of

ITALIAN TROOPS ON A TRANSPORT BOUND FOR GALLIPOLI

"On April 24 [1915], Italy at last made her arrangements with the Allies and on May 3 denounced the Triple Alliance. . . . The country was seized by a patriotic emotion which can hardly be paralleled in history. . . . On May 23 Italy was at war with Austria." This, however, was too late to allow of very effective participation in the campaign at Gallipoli.

ITALIAN ALPINI, SHORTLY AFTER SUNRISE, TOILING UP A MOUNTAIN PASS ON SKIS

ITALIAN INFANTRY ADVANCING IN AN ATTACK

Regulation steel helmets have displaced the picturesque feather-crowned caps once so familiar to Italian tourists

AN ITALIAN OFFICER'S HEADQUARTERS
This eyrie is built into the solid face of the cliff, thousands of feet up the mountain side

WATCHING THE OLD ENEMY

These Italians, at the end of one of their rocky trenches, are watching the movements of the Austrians across the valley.
It will be noted that at least three of the four soldiers are supplied with field-glasses

SNOW IN THE ITALIAN ALPS

After a heavy fall of snow it was sometimes necessary to tunnel through huge drifts like this, in order to clear the communication trenches

A BIVOUAC ON THE ISONZO

This little town in Austrian territory having been captured after a heavy bombardment, these Italian infantrymen have entered it to take possession and—they hope—to rest

ANTI-AIRCRAFT GUN ON A MOUNTAIN TOP

ITALIAN ANTI-AIRCRAFT GUNS

A vigilant watch for enemy aircraft is maintained by land and sea. Showing a gun mounted on a summit in the Italian Alps, 8,100 feet above sea-level. A glimpse of the queer-looking craft used in the anti-aircraft motor-boat patrol

THE MOUNTAIN RAMPARTS GUARDING THE ITALIAN PLAIN

An Italian signal outpost commanding a bird's-eye view of the valley thousands of feet below.   The canvas-covered
object behind the sand bags is a powerful searchlight

the British Expeditionary Army which fought about Ypres was practically exterminated. The Seventh Division alone lost 356 out of 400 officers and 9,664 out of 12,000 rank and file. At Ypres alone the British losses were 40,000. The German loss has been placed as high as 250,000 and certainly exceeded the loss at the Marne. For three weeks the British fought an enemy five times as numerous and equipped with heavy artillery and machine guns, both of which weapons were lacking to the British in any useful number. Probably 60 per cent.—perhaps more—of the British army were killed, wounded, or captured, but in the end they still held Ypres and the lines before it. For such an achievement all praise is inadequare. And at Ypres Britain's professional army perished but its tradition became thenceforth imperishable. Unlike the Spartans, who died in defeat, the British army had held its gate.

## IV.  THE SECOND BATTLE OF YPRES

The close of the First Battle of Ypres saw the Allies holding one of the most remarkable positions in all the front from Belfort to Nieuport. Pushed eastward from Ypres was a sausage-shaped salient or bulge, extending north-northeast to its greatest depth at Grafenstafel, six miles from Ypres. The base of this salient was the Ypres-Commines-Yser Canal and between the two points where the German line touched the canal, north and south of Ypres, was barely seven miles. South of this canal possession of the Messines and Wytschaete hills gave the Germans direct observation and splendid artillery sweep of the whole rear of the salient. But north of the canal the British still clung to the western slope of the ridge, from the vicinity of Gheluvelt to a point east of Zonnebeke, and from Zonnebeke westward they held both the Grafenstafel and Pilkem ridges as far as the western limits of Langemarck. Between Langemarck and the canal at Steenstrate a division of French Colonials was in line.

In April, 1915, the British were preparing for their subsequent offensive southward near La Bassée. The French had recalled their best troops from this front to participate in Foch's great Artois operation, and most of the few heavy British guns had likewise gone south. There was no expectation of any considerable German operation in the Ypres sector and Allied journals were heralding the coming of the spring offensive, which was to throw the Germans out of France and Belgium. Toward the last of the third week in April an attack, preceded by the explosion of a mine, had given the British a brief hold on Hill No. 60, a mound near the point where the Ypres-Commines Canal crossed the battle-front. Heavy attack and counter-attack on this point occupied the attention of the world in the next few days.

But on April 22 came one of the most dramatic and terrible episodes of the war. Toward evening the Germans suddenly loosed vast quantities of chlorine gas against the French Colonial division standing between Langemarck and the Ypres-Yser Canal at Steenstrate. The result was a natural and inevitable panic. The black troops fled south and west, toward Ypres and across the canal. Within a brief period the Allied front was broken and for four miles between Langemarck and the canal there was a gap. The German road to Ypres was at last open.

East of the Colonials were the Canadians. When the French troops fled, the Canadian flank was left in the air, while the Canadians were themselves exposed to gas fumes and suffered severe losses from this cause. Yet, despite all the circumstances, the Canadians hung on. They drew back their left flank, forming in a half circle, and fought on, holding up for many hours the onrush of the Germans. Here, on this front, the Canadian contingent won their title to rank with the old British Army which had held the Ypres position in the autumn and with their Anzac brethren, who were soon to win equal glory at Gallipoli.

The next morning, Friday, April 23, the situation was critical in the extreme. The Germans had forced the crossing of the Yser Canal between Boesinghe and Steenstrate and taken Lizerne, while they were in possession of Langemarck and Pilkem and crowding down the roads from these towns toward Ypres itself. Could they push on for but three miles more, Ypres would be in their hands and all the troops in the salient east of Ypres would be caught like rats in a trap. That they did not do this can only in part be credited to the bravery of the Canadians and their British supports.   In point of fact the true explanation appears to be that the Germans had not expected so tremendous a success and lacked reserves at the decisive point at the favourable moment.   A better chance than the British had had at Neuve Chapelle therefore slipped through their fingers.

In the next few days the situation slowly improved, although it remained critical during the first days of May.   First the French threw the Germans back to the east bank of the canal.   At the same time the British brought up troops from all points of their line and closed the gap between the canal and the flank of the Canadians.   Even the Belgians from their side of the Yser River sent over reinforcements.   Meantime German heavy artillery destroyed the beautiful buildings of Ypres, till then little injured, and the British army suffered from shell fire as it had not suffered even in the first days of the battle about Ypres in the preceding year.   To this heavy gun-fire it had neither the artillery nor the ammunition to make answer.

By the first of May, the day on which the Germans were to win their great victory of the Dunajec, it was plain that the old Ypres salient could no longer be held.   It had become a rectangle three miles wide by six long, thrust forth into the German lines.   From the Pilkem Ridge as well as the Messines-Wytschaete Ridge the Germans had now a sweep over British communications.   Accordingly in the second week of May the British sullenly drew back from the Grafenstafel Ridge, from Zonnebeke, from all the ridge between the Roulers Railroad and the Menin Road, and occupied a new front in a narrow semicircle rather more than a mile east of Ypres.

Almost all the high ground was now lost.   All the salvage of the First Battle of Ypres, defended with such great gallantry and obstinacy, was surrendered.   Second Ypres had been far more costly than the First in territory given up, although it must be remembered that for this the British were not responsible.   It was the collapse of the French, under the first gas attack of the war, which precipitated the disaster. Yet even this was a small solace for the Allied publics, which had expected news of a great victory both in the east and in the west and in the same hour read of the Dunajec and the surrender of all the ground memorable in the First Battle of Ypres.

By May 13 the Second Battle of Ypres closed. The German purpose had been accomplished; there had been greater success than in the earlier attack, but the purpose of the April operation was far less colossal than that of the October campaign. Then the road to Calais had been sought. Now the Germans aimed merely to weaken the Allied offensive to the southward by drawing from it men, munitions, and guns. They sought also to impress the neutral nations—Italy most of all—with their great strength on both fronts. This strength was proven, but Italy was already lost and the use of the poison gas served to arouse the indignation of men of all nations outside the Central Alliance. It was one more circumstance in the indictment of Germany by civilization. After Ypres, quarter was neither given nor taken for many months on the Flanders front and before very long the Germans, in their turn, were compelled to endure the suffering incident to a gas attack.

Without the gas the German success would have been unlikely. As it was, the success was limited and the moral consequences evil in the extreme for the Germans. The sinking of the *Lusitania* while the Second Battle of Ypres was still proceeding was instantly associated in all minds with the crime of the poison gas. And just as the Zeppelins were the best recruiting agency in Britain, German savagery roused Canada to new effort and in the first three years of the war more than 400,000 Canadians crossed the sea to fight in Flanders and Artois.

Such, briefly, is the history of the origin and development of the Ypres salient. In the First Battle of Ypres the Germans, attacking east of the town, mainly on either side of the Menin Road, gained the hills of Wytschaete and Messines. In the Second they took the Pilkem Ridge at the other side of the salient. Thenceforth they held it as in a vise between these two ridges until June and August, 1917, when the British first retook Wytschaete and Messines and then, with the aid of French divisions, swept the Germans off the Pilkem Ridge, retook Pilkem, Bixschoote, Langemarck, and St. Julien, and thus abolished the whole salient.    Until this time the Ypres salient remained the worst point on the whole Allied front, and for a long period there was a sharp debate in British military circles as to the advisability of holding Ypres or retiring to the hills behind it, Scharpenberg and Kemmel.

Ypres was not evacuated mainly because of the moral value that attached to it as a result of the two great battles.    Only Verdun could rival the old Flemish citadel, now gone to dust and ashes, in sentimental value in the first three years of the war, and the return of the British to the offensive in this region in the fourth year of the struggle made it probable that Ypres will remain for the British and the Canadian public the greatest incident in the war.    Even the Australians, who came to Flanders ultimately and rewon Zonnebeke and its surrounding woods in the last days of September, 1917, will probably rank it with Gallipoli, and thus Ypres will retain a place in British Imperial history above all other battlefields, for here the solidarity of that Empire Germany sought to destroy was proven by its sons from all the lands about the Seven Seas.

# CHAPTER ELEVEN

# THE WESTERN OFFENSIVES

## I

### GERMANY'S WESTERN STRATEGY

German strategy in the west in the summer and autumn was simple. German High Command had calculated that British preparations would not between spring and winter enable the British to make an effective attack upon the narrow front which they held. They calculated rightly that the transfer of men and munitions to Sir Ian Hamilton at Gallipoli would leave Sir John French powerless to do more than make brave but useless attacks in Flanders and Artois. The world believed that Kitchener's "Million" was a fact and that British preparations had already reached a point where Britain was a peril to the Germans. The Germans not only knew that Britain was not ready in May, 1915, but already guessed that Britain would not be ready in February, 1916. Knowing this Germany could undertake the Russian operation in 1915 and begin her preparations for the subsequent Verdun operation.

As to the French, the Germans rightly perceived that France was becoming dangerous and that the reorganization of French armies and the similar reorganization of French industry were proceeding apace. Yet they estimated that the French would be unable alone to make a breach in the German lines before the Russian campaign had been completed. They multiplied their machine guns and heavy artillery on the western front. They transformed their old trenches into double and triple lines of positions. They constructed dugouts and permanent works in cement. From the North Sea to Switzerland the German line became a veritable fortress.

Having done this the German High Command turned its back on the west and went to Russia. It left great and powerful armies behind. No large number of divisions were taken from the west to the east, but practically all the reserves available were marked for eastern use. It became the mission of the German armies in the west to hold on as best they could, even if they had to give over a certain amount of ground. Germany gambled with the Allies of the west that despite all their efforts she could hold her western front and at the same time deal Russia a crushing blow. In this she reversed the venture of August and September, 1914, when she sought to crush France while "containing" Russian armies.

And Germany won the gamble. Nor was she ever in very grave danger of losing, despite the terrific struggles of Loos and Champagne in the autumn and the only less considerable French operation in Artois in May and June. The reason of German success was that German High Command had better read the future than French or British. Germany had not expected to see her great drive at Paris end in the trenches above Soissons. She had not calculated that her tremendous push for Calais and the Channel would terminate in the trenches about Ypres. But German soldiers had studied both the Boer and the Manchurian wars. They had seen the possibilities of trench warfare and Germany had provided herself with the weapons which enabled her, standing on the defensive, to beat off her foes.

Alone of the contestants, Germany had perceived the value of the machine gun and she had thousands where her foes had scores. Her heavy artillery had been designed for a war of movement, but in the war of position it enabled her to destroy her opponents' trenches with high-explosive shells, while British shrapnel proved all but useless in preparing an attack. In addition, German troops were provided with trench mortars and hand grenades, while the British were still making their bombs of jam tins and British and French armies were without trench mortars.

To her foresight as to weapons, to her industry and skill in fortification, Germany owed her successful stand on the western front in the critical summer of 1915 when a break in the west would have meant something approaching ruin, for her main forces were committed to the eastern operation and her reserves were consumed in this great effort.

From the outbreak of the war to the Battle of the Somme this mechanical and technical advantage remained with the Germans, although in a rapidly declining measure. At Verdun the French were still inferior in heavy guns as late as July, 1916, but with the Somme, Germany loses her initial advantage permanently on the west front.

Once more, as in the case of the Russian campaign, it is necessary to recall that the contemporary judgment upon the Allied offensive of the west was entirely wrong. The German purpose was completely realized during the period from May to October, 1915. Allied gains in trenches and positions were unimportant. The much-praised victories of the Champagne and Loos had no valuable consequences. They won guns, prisoners, a few square miles of French territory, but they did not break the German line nor save Russia from the defeat which brought eventual ruin after revolution. They did not even prevent the Balkan thrust, following the gigantic Russian operation.

## II.  SPRING AND SUMMER

In the last days of April, just before the Dunajec, Germany had attacked west of Ypres, using "poison gas" for the first time and temporarily breaking the Anglo-French lines at the point where the armies of the two nations made contact. All through the first week of May the conflict about the old Flemish town was bitter. But it is plain that the Germans did not intend any new bid for the road to Calais. They sought rather to forestall the Anglo-French offensive which was preparing to the south.

In this, so far as British participation was concerned, they achieved success. When, on May 8 and 9, the great French spring offensive was launched by Foch south of La Bassée, the British share was minor. On May 9 a British operation east of Festubert brought nearly 8,000 casualties in a few hours, because there was lacking ammunition for a proper preparation. After but forty minutes of bombardment the British infantry left their trenches. Such bravery only made the losses greater and Field Marshal Sir John French, returning from the field where he had seen his soldiers slaughtered, met a despatch from the British War

Office asking him to send back 20 per cent. of his reserve ammunition for use at Gallipoli.

The result was the famous shell scandal. Sir John French put the facts of the army condition in the hands of the Conservative members of Parliament, of Lloyd George, and of Lord Northcliffe, who forthwith gave them to the world in the London *Times*. For months French had asked Kitchener for high explosives and had received shrapnel. He had asked for great amounts of munitions and he had seen his guns starved and his men slaughtered because they were without artillery support. Festubert was an unimportant skirmish on the military side, but its political effect in Britain was enormous.

Meantime Foch, attacking on the front of some dozen miles from before Lens to the western environs of Arras, made immediate and considerable gains. The value of Neuve Chapelle had been that it had demonstrated that the German line could be pierced. The attack on that occasion had opened the road to Lille. Only the failure of supports to arrive had allowed the Germans time to restore their shattered front. Thus Foch could hope to do what the British had almost accomplished. In point of fact there was a penetration of the German lines again, but it was impossible to take full advantage because the penetration was only on a narrow front. The main attack was made on the easternmost foothills of the Artois highlands, which near Lens and Arras break down abruptly into the great plain of northern France. The German line clung to the first of these hills, the ridge of Notre Dame de Lorette to the north and of the Vimy Ridge to the south.

In the first days of fighting the French cleared the Lorette Ridge. They took a number of villages toward Arras—Carency, Ablain, Souchez. They mastered the famous German fortification of the Labyrinth, just west of the Vimy Ridge. But in the end the German line held. Advancing at first after great artillery preparation the French captured positions, prisoners, and guns with small loss. But when they endeavoured to expand their gains, their losses became heavy and the prospect of real success rapidly dwindled.

By the first days of June there was a slowing down. The Battle of

Artois, the first since the end of the "Race to the Sea," had terminated in a check for the French.  Not until April, 1917, were the Allies to pass the Vimy Ridge and make good their hold on the plain below.  Before Lemberg had fallen, while the Germans were still engaged in clearing Galicia of the Russian invader, the first attempt of the western allies of Russia to relieve the pressure upon their hard-pushed comrade failed completely.  This failure left the Germans free to go on, after the Galician episode was completed, to their more considerable undertaking.  Their offensive about Ypres and the Allied drive about Lens had shown the Allies unequal to a really dangerous attack for the period of the spring and summer of 1915.

Between June and the last days of September there were various French efforts, all with only local value.  An attempt to break down the German salient about St. Mihiel failed, both when attempted south of St. Mihiel and north of Pont-à-Mousson.  A slight advance was pushed over the Vosges into the upper valley of the Fecht, west of Colmar, but it had no real value.  Actually, from June until autumn, the Allied armies stood still—gave themselves over to preparing a new attack.  While Russia perished they were still powerless to save their ally.

### III.   THE AUTUMN OFFENSIVE

It was not until September that the Allies were ready to try again.  At the moment when the Russians had won clear of the Vilna envelopment and were approaching the line upon which they were to make their final halt, Joffre and French in Artois and Champagne launched the terrific drives which were the Battles of Loos and Champagne.  Both battles were German victories, because they did not break the German lines nor compel the Germans to abandon their eastern operations.  Yet both marked real progress on the Allied side, and the French captures of prisoners in Champagne was impressive even in a war of the magnitude of the World War.

In many respects the Allied attack recalled the German strategy employed against the Warsaw salient.  In France the German line was a salient almost as sharp as that held by the Russians in the last

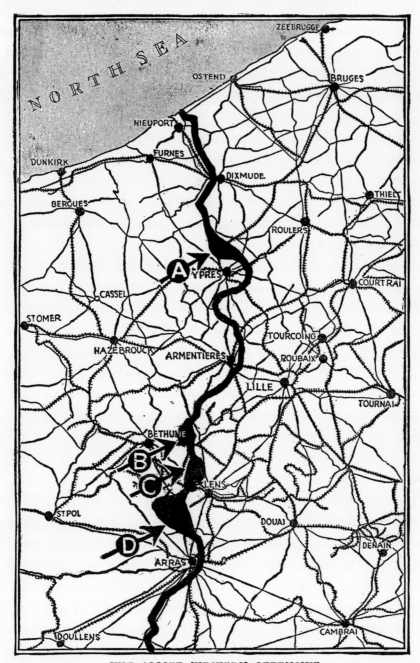

### THE ALLIED WESTERN OFFENSIVE

The scenes of the various operations between the Somme and the sea in the summer
and autumn of 1915.

*A*-The second battle of Ypres          *C*-Loos
*B*-Festubert          *D*-Foch's thrust in Artois

days of July.   From Loos to Souain the distance is about the same as from Lomza to Lublin.  A piercing of the German line both at Lens and Auberive would have produced a situation in a degree like that which existed in the east when the Germans had penetrated both sides of the Polish salient.   The Germans at Noyon, the point where the apex of the western salient approaches nearest to Paris, would have been in something of the peril of the Russians in Warsaw in the first days of August.

Thus, speaking broadly, what the Allies endeavoured to do was to attack the great German salient in France at two points well removed from the apex.   Had they been able to penetrate at both a general German retirement to the Belgian frontier would have been probable. Had either attack been successful in any but a local way, then the German salient in France would have been materially narrowed and sharpened and German communications would have been considerably, if not fatally, crippled.

In this September attack, the fronts chosen for attack were in Champagne and Artois.   Both had been the scene of desperate fighting in the spring.   In Champagne, between the Moronviller Heights, which rise a few miles to the east of Rheims and dominate the plain, and the Argonne on a front of rather less than eighteen miles, over ground which presented no great obstacle, the French chose to make their main thrust. It was historic ground.   A few miles to the south the Hunnish hordes of Attila had been routed.   Valmy, which delivered France from another Prussian invasion, was almost within sight of the new battlefield.   In Artois, west of Lens and the Vimy Ridge, the British under Sir John French, the French under Foch, were to make a new effort to get the greatest French coal city.   Lens was the immediate object of the Anglo-French attack.   Vouziers, behind the German lines and a nodal point for roads and railways alike, was the objective of the Champagne effort.

For the two drives there was an artillery preparation unequalled hitherto in the west.   In Champagne railroads had been constructed, roads built, enormous engineering work done to make possible the great bombardment, which was to surpass the Dunajec as the Dunajec had surpassed the British drum-fire at Neuve Chapelle. All the ammunition manufactured by the newly organized French industrial establishments and husbanded during the summer was now available. The French armies had been reorganized, newly equipped. No French army was ever in better spirits and in a better state of preparation than that

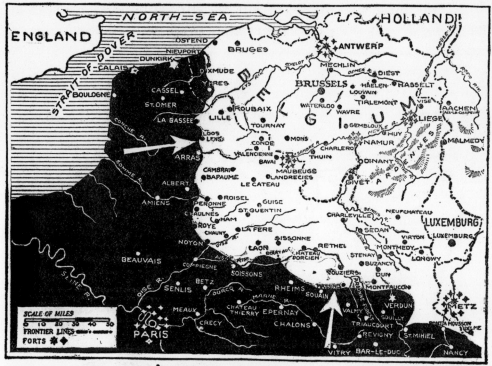

THE ALLIES' AUTUMN OFFENSIVE IN THE WEST, 1915

The arrows show locations of the British operations about Lens, and of the French campaign in Champagne. In many respects the Allied attack recalled the German strategy successfully employed against the Warsaw salient during the previous summer. (See map on page 152.)

which under Pétain, soon to command the attention of the world as the defender of Verdun, made the great venture of September 25, 1915.

Nor was Foch's army less worthy of the best traditions of the French. Its commander had delivered the decisive thrust at the Marne, after having saved the beaten army of Lorraine in the retreat from Morhange. His victory at the Yser had saved Calais—and in the winning of it he had been decisively aided by the British, who remained associated with him in the new campaign. Even the fighting of May and June had disclosed Foch as a great master of trench warfare, although he lacked the

guns and munitions to win a real victory.   After three years of war
Foch and Pétain were to remain the two great fighters on the French
side when Joffre had gone, and it is worthy of note that we see them
now at last, one commanding a group of armies, the other the army that
made the great drive in Champagne.

By the third week of September the preparations were complete.
By September 20 the guns were roaring in the greatest bombardment

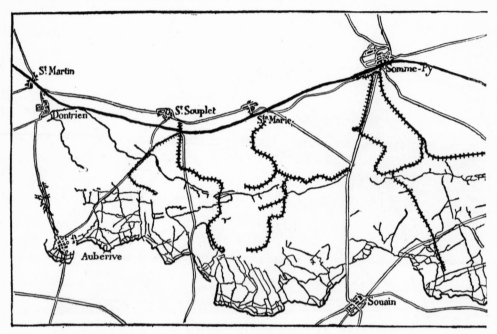

MAP OF GERMAN TRENCHES AT CHAMPAGNE—WESTERN HALF
This map and the one opposite are reproduced from one prepared by the French General Staff.  They show
the system of German trenches assaulted by the French, September 25, 1915

of the war, the fire beginning along the whole front and gradually concentrating in the narrow sectors which were to see the real attack.   The
guns gave the Germans full warning of what was to come, but there was
no need of warning for the Germans were already fully aware of the
preparations being made.

### IV.   CHAMPAGNE

On the morning of September 25, just as daylight broke, the French
left their trenches between Souain and Massiges on a front of more than

fifteen miles and advanced in successive waves against the German lines. On the western flank of the attack, about Souain, they had before them only rolling country, destitute of cover—the familiar sterile and monotonous chalk plain of the "Dusty Champagne." In the centre the ground was broken by bits of woodland and by more considerable hills. On the extreme east the ground before the French was much higher and more difficult and culminated in that oddly shaped elevation

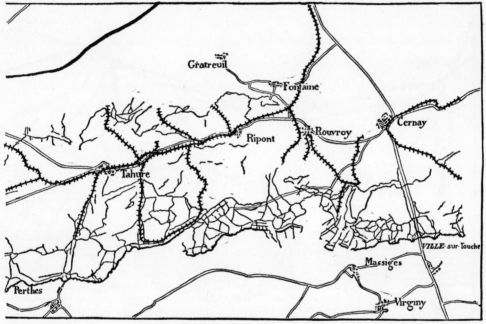

MAP OF GERMAN TRENCHES AT CHAMPAGNE—EASTERN HALF

The curling, twisting, tentacle-like railroads that seem to end nowhere are narrow-gauge lines built by the Germans for the purpose of serving their trenches

called by the soldier the "hand" of Massiges because on the map its outline resembled that of a hand with clearly defined fingers.

The artillery preparation had been so complete that the French crossed the first system of German trenches with small loss in almost all sectors. Only here and there were they held up, chiefly in the centre, by machine guns hidden in underbrush and by concrete defenses of the sort which the British "Tommy" later named "pill-boxes." But the effect of the partial checks along the front was to give the advance a wholly irregular outline. It had started as a great wave, moving in perfect alignment at a given moment.    But by afternoon it resembled the toothed edge of a handsaw.

For a great success it was essential that the weather should be clear and thus the field of observation for the aëroplanes unobstructed.   But before noon rain began to fall, transforming the chalk soil into mud, making observation next to impossible at the precise moment when it was essential that the guns should be brought to bear upon the various German defences of the first line and its support trenches which had survived the first drum-fire.   At the moment of victory the French advance now began to slow down.

The next day the attack was resumed.   The whole of the German first line was methodically reduced, but the Germans had learned their lesson at the Dunajec and behind the first line was a second, not nearly so strong, but strong enough to hold, particularly as the French artillery had to be moved forward to reach it.   Yet the French did at some points breach the second line.   A Moroccan brigade north of Souain actually won clear of the whole German position, only to be annihilated by the concentrated fire of the guns behind the German trenches.

Meantime the Germans had begun to draw reserves from all portions of their western front.   They seem to have had no real strategic reserve for portions of more than fifty different commands were presently identified.   Men and guns arrived from all sides and the German second line still held.   Moreover, the French, having won their first advance with small loss, were beginning to pay heavy prices for each new foot gained. The old experience of Neuve Chapelle and Artois was being repeated. Already it was clear that the Dunajec triumph was not to be duplicated.

Wherefore, in the first days of October, the French determined to "cut their losses"—to take such profit as they had made and abandon all effort to get more.   They had now advanced on a front of fifteen miles on an average above a mile and a half and at points more than two miles.   They had taken more than 25,000 prisoners and 150 field and heavy guns, together with an enormous booty of munitions and small arms.   It was a bigger bag of guns and prisoners than Napoleon had won at Jena or at Austerlitz and not since 1806 had any Prussian army shown

# GALLIPOLI

THE LANDING OF THE AUSTRALIANS AT ANZAC BEACH, GALLIPOLI

"The landing was one of the ghastliest incidents of the whole war. For a month the Turks had been preparing. Not only was the shore fortified, but the beaches, the shallows were covered by submerged barbed wires. Against this position the British were sent in open boats, partly but not effectively covered by the fire of the fleet. They made the landing . . . but not less than 15,000 casualties was the price of the effort. As many troops as the United States sent to Cuba in the first Santiago expedition were killed, wounded, or captured on this first day [April 25, 1915] of the Gallipoli fighting."

## BRITISH BLUEJACKETS COMING ASHORE AT MUDROS

Sir Ian Hamilton's force for the Gallipoli campaign was mobilized in Egypt and transported to Mudros Bay, on the Island of Lemnos, which lies in the Ægean opposite the entrance to the Dardanelles and about fifty miles away

## AT CAPE HELLAS

View from a British officer's dugout on the cliffs. The splash in the middle distance was made by a Turkish shell which passed over the photographer's head and fell uncomfortably near the transports lying at anchor. The main British force landed near this point—at the toe of the boot—and was never able to advance farther than three miles from here.

A SANDBAG RAMPART FOR THE PROTECTION OF THE AUSTRALIANS AT ANZAC BEACH

The tragedy of Gallipoli was the hopelessness of it all.  "Never in British history was there a more splendid example of the tenacity and the courage which have made the great empire.   Nothing in English or world history surpasses this devotion of the men of Britain, of Australia, and of New Zealand, fighting under conditions beyond belief, enduring hardships  beyond  exaggeration."

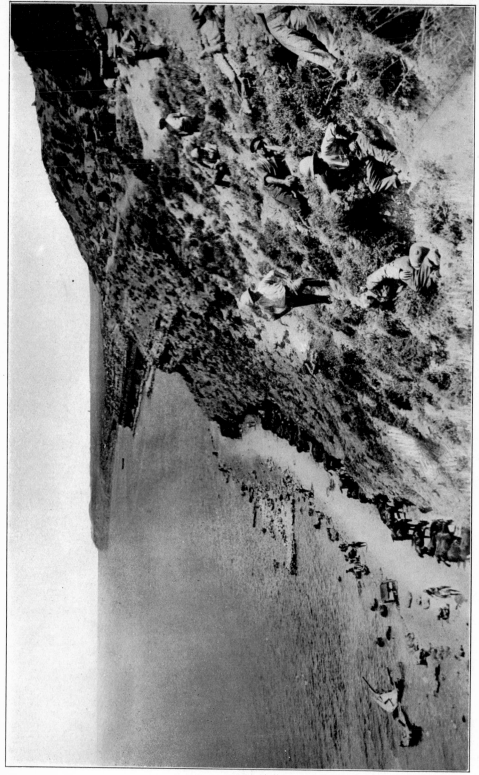

A DARDANELLES HEADLAND

"The whole area was a series of confused gullies, steep hills, and deep ravines. . . . The climatic conditions were indescribably bad. In winter the peninsula was swept by the cold blasts from the Black Sea. In summer it was baked by a tropical sun which dried up all the water courses and turned the country into a desert and a furnace. All water for drinking purposes had to be brought from Egypt or Lemnos."

A BRITISH CAMP ON THE SUN-BAKED PENINSULA

"No movement could be made without first advertising its character by preparations carried out under Turkish eyes. A more helpless, hapless position for a great army cannot be imagined, nor is there anything in military history since the Crimea to compare with the hardships of the men of Gallipoli"

A TURKISH STRONGHOLD

The interior of one of the Turkish strongholds during a heavy bombardment. Looking out to sea, the smoke-clouded Allied fleet is just visible

A FRENCH RECONNAISSANCE

A well-aimed Turkish shell has just exploded on the right. Two men are seen crawling toward positions of comparative safety behind a sandy rampart which a third has reached

THE END, AT GALLIPOLI

Their stores at Suvla Bay were set afire by the British when the hapless enterprise was finally abandoned.
In December German successes in the Balkans opened the road between Turkey and her great ally and insured the speedy arrival of German artillery at Gallipoli.
Evacuation became inevitable, and on December 19 the troops were withdrawn from Suvla.

such readiness to surrender in detail. Of course there was no surrender of large units. As to losses, that of each side certainly passed 100,000; the French was approximately 120,000; the German materially greater.

In the moral sense the French were therefore justified in claiming the Champagne as a victory. The sight of the thousands of German prisoners, the parks of Prussian cannon in the courtyard of the Invalides in Paris, the stories of German troops surrendering, all contributed to raise the spirits of the French people and break the long period of depression which had come after the spring efforts had failed and the Russian defeats had demonstrated that France was not to be liberated from the invader during the current year. Artois had been in a measure a cause for optimism in the spring, but the Champagne was in much greater degree a cause for rejoicing.

Yet it is plain that considerable as was the local and tactical success in Champagne, it did not affect the main issue or modify the German purpose. Some German divisions were rushed back from the east. The extreme objectives of the Germans in Russia were not all reached. There was a prompt reduction of pressure upon Russia. But the western offensive came too late to save Russia, now doomed to fall to Revolution and subsequent military powerlessness, and it did not force the Germans to give over their Balkan plans now maturing.

## V. LOOS

The Artois operation was entirely subsidiary. The Allies, unlike the Germans, did not attempt to break the hostile salient on both sides. Their hope was to smash it in Champagne and by pressure in Artois prevent the enemy from sending troops from west to east. Hence there was no large expectation and no adequate preparation, particularly on the part of the British, for a real success. And, as it happened, when the British did break the German line, they were totally unable to turn to permanent advantage a success which, for the moment, promised greater real profit than was attained by the army either of Pétain in Champagne or of Foch in Artois.

The Artois operation was assigned to the northernmost army of the group commanded by Foch and the southernmost army of French, which was commanded by Sir Douglas Haig. The immediate objective of the French was the Vimy Ridge, the last highland of the Artois Plateau, which breaks down sharply into the plain east of the Vimy Hills. The British aimed at the German lines covering the great road which runs north from Lens to La Bassée over high ground. The only considerable village in the British sector was that of Loos, two miles northwest of Lens and situated just at the western slope of Hill No. 70, which dominates Lens from the north. The French attacked upon a front of rather less than ten miles; the operative front of the British was hardly half as wide.

The French attack was successful and on September 25 and the succeeding days they pushed to the top of the Vimy Ridge, but were unable to clear the summit. In some places the Germans held the eastern slope, the French the western, and the crest was a "No-man's land." There was a moment when it seemed that the whole ridge would be won, but the British to the north became involved in difficulties which made it necessary for the French to go to their assistance and abandon their own operation. The result was that Vimy was only half taken and later in the war, when the British took over this sector from the French, a German attack won back much of the lost ground. It was not until Easter Monday, April 9, 1917, that the Canadians were to clear Vimy of its German garrisons.

Turning now to the British attack, the problem was this: The ground rolled gently upward from the British and was seamed with German trenches, two complete systems interposing between the British and the Lens-La Bassée highroad. The main obstacles were found in the coal pits and slag heaps—the characteristic features of the whole Lens district. The northernmost of the British attacks was aimed at the famous Hohenzollern Redoubt, just south of the La Bassée Canal; the southernmost at the village of Loos, with Hill No. 70 behind it as an ultimate objective. Various defensive works between these two points along the highway were the objectives of the centre.

The British attack got away handsomely after the customary bombardment at daylight on September 25. In the early hours the success was complete. The Hohenzollern Redoubt was captured, the works covering the highway were reached and taken, and the highway crossed at various points. But the great triumph was to the south, where the Highlanders took Loos, pushed on and captured the redoubt and slopes of Hill 70, and pressed on over the eastern slope of the hill. A great success was now within sight. The last German trench line had been penetrated. The Germans were hastily moving their heavy guns out of Lens and the evacuation of the town had begun.

But again, at the critical moment, the British staff broke down. The success was out of proportion to the expectation. Such immediate reserves as were available—two divisions of the new army—were pushed up, but under the strain they broke down and fled, repeating the performance of the French Fifteenth Army Corps at Morhange. The Scottish troops had neglected to disarm and send to the rear the garrison of the redoubt on Hill 70 and these troops now took up their arms and reoccupied their old fort. Not until midsummer, 1917, were the British again to occupy this height.

From the afternoon of September 25 until the morning of September 27 there was a chance that the great success might be made permanent, but, just as at Neuve Chapelle and Suvla, the golden opportunity passed. The Scottish troops were either destroyed or pushed back from their vantage points, Hill 70 was retaken by the Germans, who again pushed west of the Lens-La Bassée highroad. By September 27 their line was restored, their counter-attacks were beginning to threaten the safety of the British, and Sir John French had to appeal to Foch for assistance. The lines became stationary again. The thing that happened in Champagne also occurred in Artois. In both places the Germans had lost ground, but had preserved the continuity of their front and parried a deadly thrust.

At Loos the British took 3,000 prisoners and twenty-five guns. They lost rather more than 60,000 men—a loss greater than the combined casualty lists of the Northern and Southern armies at Gettysburg.

Their gain in ground was nowhere much deeper than a mile and over a front of less than four miles.   And within a brief time the British realized that another great opportunity had been missed.   Neuve Chapelle, Loos, Suvla Bay—these are all illuminating examples of the cost to a nation of unpreparedness and the fallacy of the notion that armies can be improvised or staffs created when the fact of war has surprised a nation totally unready.

Loos sealed the fate of Sir John French.   His return to England was there assured, although it did not come for several months.   It is probably true that the chief blame rested upon the nation which had failed in peace to prepare for war.   The main faults of Loos were the faults incident to just such an army as Britain had been compelled to improvise.   Yet it is hard not to believe that a portion of the blame rested with the commander-in-chief in the field.   In a few months after Loos, French gave way to his immediate lieutenant, Sir Douglas Haig, while Sir William Robertson became chief of staff and there was a consequent reorganization of the whole British military establishment.

Thus, in a sense, Loos marks the lowest point in British military tide during the first three years of the war, although the evacuation of Gallipoli and the surrender at Kut-el-Amara, which came later, were evidences of the same conditions.   On the morrow of Loos the German General Staff could justly calculate that Russia had fallen and Britain had failed.   France alone could not pierce the German lines on the offensive.   Could she, on the defensive, resist the German attack, still deprived of effective aid from Britain?   The German officers decided not and we may see in the result of Loos a strong stimulus toward the Verdun attack that was to come a few months later.   At Ypres in April, at Loos in September, Germany had tested British strength; both tests had proven satisfactory to the Teutonic mind.   If Germany had failed to dispose of France at the Marne and by a single blow, she had now disposed of Russia and could risk another blow at France, before Britain could arrive.   Loos, after all, was the preface to Verdun.

## VI.  ITALIAN OFFENSIVES

To complete the story of western offensives during the campaign
of 1915 it is now necessary to glance at the Italian operations.  When
Italy entered the war the Allies promptly expected great results with
brief delays.  That Italy would take Trieste, break through the narrow
gap between the Adriatic and the Julian Alps, and follow the route by

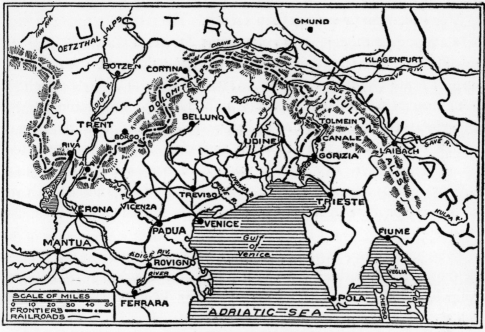

### THE ITALIAN FRONTIER

As soon as the Italians entered the war they swarmed over the frontier north of Verona and west of
Gorizia, and took Cortina and a few other towns outside the Austrian fortifications.  But they nowhere
penetrated Austrian territory twenty miles, and as soon as they came within range of heavy artillery, fixed
behind permanent trenches, they themselves were forced to take to earth.  The Italian campaign of 1915
thenceforward continued to be an affair of trench warfare.

which the young Napoleon in 1797 reached the Semmering Pass and
grasped the key to Vienna, seemed assured.

But once more, as so frequently in this fatal year, Paris, London, and
Petrograd quite ignored the facts.  When the World War began, trench
conflict was still unexpected and for the first two months the war moved
down into France and then back toward Belgium with such campaigning as had been looked for before the struggle opened.  The first battles
were analogous to those of 1870.  The Marne was still a battle of movement.  It was only at the Aisne that war of position began.

In the Italian campaign the war started in the trenches. Austria, long aware of the menace of Italian preparation, began early to construct trenches along her whole western front, from Switzerland to the Adriatic. For months the work went on. Thus when Italy at last struck, she ran her head instantly against long lines of prepared positions, such as those in France and Belgium had become. She was halted, and the third anniversary of the war found her still held between the Julian Alps and the Gulf of Trieste.

In the very first days of their war the Italians swarmed over the frontier north of Verona and west of Gorizia; they took Cortina, Ala, Gradisca, and a few other towns outside the trace of Austrian fortifications. Nowhere did they get twenty miles into Austrian territory; nowhere did they make any real breach in the trenches the Austrians had prepared. Like the French and the British advancing from the Marne to the Aisne, they suddenly came within range of heavy artillery, fixed behind permanent trenches, well prepared. And, like the French and the British, they were forced to take to earth.

This is the story of the Italian campaign of 1915. Along most of the front from Lago di Garda to the lower valley of the Isonzo the Italians were operating in a region of great mountains, some of them rising to 10,000 feet. The summits, the foothills, all the roads and approaches had long been covered by Austrian defences. There was little chance to blast a way through this barrier; there was none to rush it. Slow, steady pressure, the capture of a summit here, a trench there; a difficult and tedious effort—not to break through, but, on this front, merely to dig in so firmly that if the Germans should join the Austrians in a drive into Italy the Italian position would hold. This was, and for two years and a half remained, the Italian campaign. Remember that this frontier was traced by Austrian military engineers intent on keeping for Austria every military vantage point, and the Italian task is comprehensible.

Between the Adriatic and the mountains, along the Isonzo River, there is a district of relatively level character perhaps thirty miles broad. This is the Gorizia front. Here the Italians could undertake precisely the operation the French twice attempted in Champagne.

By concentrating heavy artillery here they might hope to blast a way into Austria. In the month of November they made the greatest of their many attempts, striving to exert a pressure that would prevent the Austrians from detaching troops to help the Germans in Serbia, as the English and French in Champagne and Loos had sought to relieve the Russians.

But, despite the repeated attacks—and the Austrians conceded that both infantry and artillery played a desperate part—Gorizia was not taken, the Austrian line held, the Italians were checked with losses estimated by the Austrians at 150,000. Italy gained trenches, as France did in Champagne, although she took no such bag of guns and prisoners; but the Isonzo line held.

The French and British hopes of victory in the west were shattered at Champagne and Loos. Their expectation of an early and decisive success by the Italians over Austria was soon shown to be futile. Italy did not by her entrance save Russia; she did not immediately endanger Austria; she could not even exert enough pressure to prevent the destruction of Serbia in the autumn. What was far worse, from the Italian point of view, the campaigns of 1915 and 1917 did not clear the Austrians out of Trent and the great salient, which, like an enormous cape, projected into the Venetian plain.

Until this great bastion was taken Italy must always face the danger of a sudden thrust south, either through the valley of the Brenta, the valley of the Adige, or along the shores of Lago di Garda. Such a thrust, if it reached the plain, would envelop all the Italian armies between the Brenta and the Isonza and threaten one of the greatest disasters in military history. Despite all her exertions Italy could not bar this road in 1915, and the spring of 1916 was to bring a grave menace in the Austrian offensive which sought to reach the plain by the Brenta valley and did almost succeed while November and December of 1917 were to bring still deadlier peril from the same direction.

Like Britain and France, then, Italy failed to get forward in 1915. Like France she was now soon to be menaced by a deadly peril already preparing behind the screen of the Dolomites, as the Verdun drive was being organized in the forests east of the Meuse fortress. In Artois, in Champagne, in Trent, and on the Isonzo, the Central Powers had made good their defensive, while disposing of Russia. They were to maintain their lines successfully now, while Serbia was destroyed and the road to the Golden Horn and the Persian Gulf flung open. Afterward it would be time to come west and strive to win the war.

# CHAPTER TWELVE

## BACK TO THE BALKANS

### I

As early as mid-July, when the Russians still held Warsaw and the real extent of the Dunajec disaster was yet unknown, there began to come from Belgrade, Bucharest, and Athens warnings that the Balkan situation was about to enter a new phase. Hardly had Warsaw fallen when the reports became more ominous, and it was no longer to be doubted that there was being organized north of the Danube and along the Serbian frontier a new Austro-German operation. Actually Mackensen was already laying the foundation for his next great campaign.

German strategy was then hidden from the Allied statesmen and generals, who were still unconscious of the true magnitude of Russian disaster and the real impotence of French and British offensive campaigns on the western front. In July, 1915, the Allied press and publics still expected the fall of Gallipoli and the successful defence of Warsaw; they were still awaiting news that should assure them of the possession of Constantinople and the end of the German blockade of Russia.

German statesmanship and High Command saw things much more clearly. It had become time to move southward. The situation in Turkey was not immediately perilous; German officers in the Sultan's service could assure the Kaiser that the lines of Gallipoli would hold; but the political conditions were such that it was plain to perceive an hour was coming when Germany would need to be represented by real force at Constantinople and at Sofia, when Athens would need a practical example of German power.

In Turkey there was a strong party which still leaned to the Allied cause. Enver had driven the nation into war, but he had not yet won any considerable triumph, apart from the defeat of the British fleet at the Straits. A Turkish army had been heavily defeated in Armenia; a British army was moving up the Tigris toward Bagdad and was still unchecked, and the British army at the Dardanelles was receiving rein-forcements and more guns and munitions.   Despite all efforts the flow of munitions from Germany and Austria to Turkey was far from ade-quate; Turkish losses were mounting rapidly; the suffering of the popula-tion of Constantinople was great; the war was becoming unpopular, and Enver was growing weaker, if not immediately in danger.

The situation in Athens, in Sofia, in Bucharest will be examined in detail presently, but it is sufficient now to point out that, while in the Greek and Bulgar capitals the influence of the Thrones still protected German interests, the conditions were such that it was unwise to post-pone too long the transformation of the promises made to the Balkan sovereigns into a reality proven by German arms.   The situation was favourable, but it was unlikely that it could forever remain favourable, for Allied diplomacy, however inept, was already beginning to pass from the domain of idealism to the region of solid fact, which alone has value in the Balkans.

With the fall of Lemberg and the expulsion of the Russians from all but a corner of the Austrian territory near the Rumanian frontier, the Rumanian problem could be adjourned.   Germany could afford to ignore Bucharest since after the Dunajec the chance of an immediate entrance of this small Latin state was slight; but Bulgaria and Greece, having goods to dispose of—armies and ships—and having ambitions which were popular as well as royal, were now pressing their wares, and if their kings were already German possessions the peoples were not.   And more than this, these peoples were quite as willing to serve the Entente as the Central Powers, provided the bribe of the former were greater than that of the latter.

In a word, the Balkan situation had now reached a stage at which, both because of diplomatic and political conditions, further German neglect might have fatal consequences.   Turkey might crack; Bulgaria, despite its king, might make a bargain with the Allies.   Venizelos might prevail over Constantine.   Enver might presently fall to an assassin and his successor restore the old situation in which British and French influence was supreme at the Golden Horn.

All this the Germans had foreseen.   As early as the days when Lemberg was falling, their attention had been turned to the Danube.   On July 17, while Warsaw was still seemingly impregnable, Germany had set her hand to a treaty with the Bulgarian Czarlet whereby, in return for the promise of Bulgarian aid, she had contracted to send an army south before Christmas.   Yet, so blind were the Allied diplomatists, that for weeks thereafter they still sought to purchase a Sovereign and a state already visibly marked "sold."

## II.  MILITARY ASPECTS

The political aspects of the new Balkan programme of the Germans were hardly less obvious than the military.   When the Allies went to the Dardanelles they had embarked upon a "sideshow" not alone foolish because it was beyond their resources, but fatal because it removed many thousands of men from the decisive field, which was the western front, and deprived them of any strategic reserve should they need it elsewhere.   The British campaign in Mesopotamia was a similar example of bad strategy, destined to have evil effect in the future no longer distant.

But a German campaign to Constantinople was another affair. Until Serbia was eliminated the Austrians would be compelled to keep large armies along the Danube and the Drina.   They were bound to watch over their Serb subjects; they were bound to suffer in the eyes of all their Slav subjects because of the two Serbian victories of Valievo and the Jedar.   But if the Germans once crushed Serbia and opened the road to Byzantium, then the mission of watching over a conquered Serbia could be confided to a Bulgar ally.   Bulgaria had the men and the material to take over the Balkan front, once Serbia was crushed.

More than this, Turkish troops, once the road to Austria was open, could be brought to the eastern front to fight against Russia, as did actually occur a year later.   They could be brought north to the Bulgar frontier to watch Rumania and to join in a general attack upon this state, if it should enter the war.   This, too, did occur in the following year and strong Turkish forces were with Mackensen when he took the Dobrudja and pushed north through Constantza to the mouths of the Danube.

When they sent their troops to the Dardanelles and Mesopotamia, the British locked them up in the peninsula, but when the Germans sent their armies to the southward they still kept them in close communication with the main masses in the east and the west. Troops from the Balkans could always be promptly recalled if necessary and sent to Galicia or Champagne with the briefest delay—a thing quite impossible in the case of the British troops at Gallipoli. But more than this, the Germans by crushing Serbia would actually make available for their own purposes both the Bulgar and the Turkish armies. Success would mean not opening a new front, but turning an old front over to new allies and in addition gaining divisions to use on the old fronts. The recruiting officer went with the conquerer on the road to the Near East.

The Bulgarian army was not under 300,000 strong. The Turks still possessed a million men under arms and very large reserves of man-power still awaiting guns and equipment. By the new campaign Germany could hope to abolish the Serbian front, releasing Austrian troops for the Italian campaign; turn over to the Bulgars any problem raised by the sending of an Allied army to Salonica, if this should occur; and still count upon Bulgar and Turkish troops to overawe Rumania, whose real hostility was never doubted in Berlin. Further than this, German guns and ammunition would enable the Turks, fighting at a disadvantage now in Mesopotamia, to turn and save Bagdad.

And beyond all these immediate possibilities loomed the larger horizon. Russia was being crushed. Her collapse was already inevitable in the German mind. Either a separate peace or a revolution would follow the campaign of 1915, the German quite correctly calculated. He would then have to deal with France, but for France he was already preparing the Verdun blow which would put the Republic out of the war, since he was satisfied that France could not successfully resist and he knew that Britain was unready.

With France and Russia out, there was left Britain. But once

German armies had opened the route to Asia Minor, the Bagdad and Hedjaz railroads pointed the way to an immediate invasion of Egypt by Suez and an eventual invasion of India by the route of Alexander the Great. Threatened in Egypt and India, deserted by French and Russian allies who had been forced by the Dunajec and a Verdun defeat separately to make peace, Britain, the Germans could expect, would abandon the battle, or, if she refused, Germany could confront with equanimity the prospect of a war with Britain alone, fought mainly by Turkish troops under German control in remote Asiatic regions, its European phase chiefly noteworthy because of the intensive submarine warfare which Germany was now considering.

And if Britain yielded, then there was left to Germany the most astounding prize of modern history—the mastery of Central Europe and of Western Asia. Indemnified by France, who would bear the costs of the war; assured on her eastern frontier against Russia by the possession of Poland, Ukraine, and the Courland; controlling Bulgaria and Greece through their kings and Turkey by her agents, Germany could adjourn her other purposes until "next time."

Never did the German genius for organization shine more brilliantly than in this Balkan episode. For just this moment Germany had been preparing for years. Her agents in all the Near East had laid the foundations of that German rule which was some day to come south across the Danube and reach Byzantium and Bagdad, Salonica and Smyrna, Suez and Basra.

The moment had now come, but the political and military aspects had both been carefully weighed. Germany had delivered the blow at Russia which was becoming effective and would presently become well-nigh fatal. She was meditating and preparing the blow against France which was to be the Verdun campaign; and in the midst of these colossal operations she was already sketching the blow against Britain, to be delivered at Suez, the Heel of the British Achilles, as German writers had long insisted.

Is it cause for wonder that the German, seeing these things face to face, made no effort to restrain his contempt for the Allied press and public men who, in the summer of 1915, were shouting about trenches gained in Artois and Champagne, prospective advances in Gallipoli and Mesopotamia, and seeking to gloss over Russian disaster by false conclusions drawn from imperfect information?

### III. THE CZAR FERDINAND

It remains now to discuss the actual Balkan facts during the period between the outbreak of the war and the moment when Bulgaria formally allied herself with the Central Powers. We may ignore the Rumanian phase because Russian diplomacy quite foolishly refused to make fair terms with the Rumanians while Russian armies were still advancing victoriously in the Carpathians, believing that Rumanian aid was unnecessary; and Rumanian statesmen, after the Russian defeats, quite wisely decided that neutrality was their only safe course. It remained so even in the subsequent summer, when the great decision was made at Bucharest. But now it is safe to say that the Allies might have had Rumania at any moment before the Dunajec, and through Russian arrogance, lost aid which would have been of incalculable advantage.

In the case of Bulgaria the Allied defeat was due to other causes. At the close of the Second Balkan War, Ferdinand, who had provoked the war at the instigation of Vienna, was saved from exile only by the financial aid given to his country by Germany and Austria. Since he was always the creature of Vienna and of Berlin this did not change his status, but it should have warned the Allies. Here was a mean, cowardly, altogether abhorrent kinglet, whose allegiance to the enemies of the Allies was based alike on fear and on selfishness, who was still the cleverest diplomatist in German pay. He had neither a sincere nor an honest thought. His character was known to all. Yet for a whole year Allied diplomacy continued to deal with this man, basing its action on the theory that he was both a patriot and a friend.

Ferdinand's subservience to the Central Powers was personal, not expressive of the will of his subjects. From the Second Balkan War Bulgaria had emerged shorn of her conquests. She had been plundered by Rumania. She had lost Macedonia to the Serbs, who had taken what, in their ante-bellum treaty, they had pledged to Bulgaria; she had lost Kavala and Drama to the Greeks after taking them; she had even lost Adrianople to the Turk. The victor of Lule Burgas, the state which had made the greatest sacrifice of all the Balkan nations, had emerged from the war the least benefited.

Now Bulgaria—every man, woman, and child in Bulgaria—was determined to abolish the iniquitous Treaty of Bucharest, to regain what she had lost, and the Bulgarian army was at the service of the Alliance which would offer this restoration. The Bulgar was quite as willing to fight the Turk as the Serb, provided that the reward were equally good, and this willingness was not based upon sordid considerations. Macedonia was his Alsace, Adrianople his Trieste, the Dobrudja a recently amputated Lorraine still bleeding.

But the difficulty within the situation lay in the fact that while the people of Bulgaria were ready to take either side, their Czar was already committed. Hence there never was any chance of winning Bulgaria to the Allied side short of eliminating Ferdinand, and this was beyond the conception, if not beyond the power, of the Allies. Instead they set out to persuade Serbia, Greece, and Rumania to restore the Bulgar's lands. Even had there been no question of bad faith this was a dangerous experiment. Serbia had rendered magnificent service to the Allied cause and in so doing suffered terribly, while the Allies had done nothing for her. It came with bad grace from London and Paris then, this appeal to Serbia to surrender what she had won at the Bregalnitza, while her great allies had still failed to open her road to the Adriatic. Once this road was open, once she had a window on the sea, she was ready to give up Monastir, but even this was not easy, for she still had a treaty with Greece which bound her to keep her contact with the state which had been her ally in the recent conflict.

Serbia, however, was the least difficult of the obstacles. The Serb might yield, but what of Greece? She had once, with bitter anguish, consented to see Kavala remain Bulgar, despite its overwhelming Greek population. But although she had agreed to this, Bulgaria had attacked her; and the atrocities of the Bulgars committed against the Hellenes of the Kavala district had roused all Greece in the Second Balkan War.

Kavala had been won, Drama and Seres had been taken by Constantine after the great victory of Kilkis.   Now the Allies, who desired Greek aid and the assistance of Greek armies, began their negotiations by calling upon Greece not to receive territory but to yield it, to surrender what she possessed against a possible future profit, after a bloody and doubtful struggle.

## IV.   CONSTANTINE AND VENIZELOS

Such a proposal as the cession of Kavala opened a new situation. The Greek King was as thoroughly committed to the German cause as Ferdinand.   His wife is the sister of the German Emperor.   He was a German Field Marshal and his military training had been German.   He had accepted the Kaiser's mediæval notions of royalty; he shared the Kaiser's hatred of the British and the French.   He believed Germany would win; he desired that she should; and he was ready at all times to aid Germany when to do so was physically possible.

All Constantine's natural sympathies were heightened by the fact that his great minister, Venizelos, was pro-Ally.   Of all the Balkan figures Venizelos alone is both great and admirable.   New Greece had been fashioned by his hands.   He had come from Crete in 1909 and saved the Hellenic State and the Danish dynasty.   He had planned the Balkan confederation which conquered the Turk.   He had organized the armies that defeated both the Osmanli and the Bulgar and gave Athens its first experience as a victorious capital in nearly twenty-five centuries. Inevitably the great minister clashed with the weak king.

Again Allied statesmanship was blind to the fact.   Venizelos was deservedly popular in Greece, but he was not an absolute master. The Greek people, having driven Constantine into exile but a few years before, were now loyal and admiring servants.   He had brought military victory.   He had expunged the shame of the earlier Turkish War.   He had defeated Turkish armies and captured Salonica and Janina.   He had routed the Bulgar hosts at Kilkis and pursued them into the remote fastnesses of the Upper Struma.

Thus, when the Allies first sent their ships to the Dardanelles, Veni-

THE RECAPTURE OF PRZEMYSL—I

A big gun used by the Germans in the siege

THE RECAPTURE OF PRZEMYSL—II

Pioneers of the Austro-German forces building a bridge over the San River near Przemysl.

On March 23, 1915, the city of Przemysl in Galicia surrendered to the Russians after a siege which had lasted 200 days, and 119,000 Austrians were taken prisoners. Ten weeks later, when the Germans had come to the aid of the Austrians, the city was recaptured after a furious assault which lasted about a week. The comparative length of the sieges is significant.

SCENES IN GALICIA AND RUSSIAN POLAND—I

A young officer of the Polish Legion cavalry troop questions a scout who has just returned from a reconnaissance

SCENES IN GALICIA AND RUSSIAN POLAND—II

A German scout finds a mortally wounded sentinel who had crawled to a stream to quench his thirst

## THE GRAND DUKE AND THE CZAR

"I hear constant talk of peace," he said. "I hear story after story that the pro-German influences at this Court are having their effects on you. I want to know if these reports are true?" (*See page 386*)

GRAND DUKE NICHOLAS, COMMANDER-IN-CHIEF OF THE RUSSIAN ARMIES, TILL
DISASTER OVERTOOK RUSSIA IN THE SUMMER OF 1915

THE GERMAN ARMY ENTERS WARSAW

On August 4, 1915, the army of Prince Leopold of Bavaria entered Warsaw, one year to a day after the British declaration of war had transformed the contest into a World War. The Battle of the Dunajec had been won on May Day; less than a hundred days later the Germans were in Warsaw. Prince Leopold is here shown reviewing his victorious troops

THE RUSSIAN IDEA OF TRANSPORT —

Unexpectedly mild weather melted snow and ice and made hard going for this transport sledge, which finally skidded sidewise into the river

BURNING OF BREST-LITOWSK

After the Russian defeat on the Dunajec, May 1, 1915, disasters came thick and fast.   To mention only a few: Warsaw was lost on August 4; Kovno on the 17th; and Brest-Litowsk had to be abandoned on the 25th.   This picture shows the burning of the stores, with citizens attempting to make salvage of some of the grain, for their private hoards

AND THE WAY THE GERMANS HANDLED IT

Miles and miles of German transport wagons creeping across the Polish plains

RUSSIAN PRISONERS CROSSING THE VISTULA

These men fought bravely, but they were betrayed by the government. Time and again at the most critical hours during 1915 ammunition failed. Hundreds of thousands of lives were sacrificed, great regions of Russia were devastated and lost, because of German intrigue in Petrograd and German influence among the reactionaries who surrounded the Czar

HORDES OF RUSSIAN PRISONERS PATIENTLY WAITING TO BE FED

"The campaign of 1915 destroyed the monarchy in the eyes of the people of Russia. . . . While the military aspect of the great Russian disaster has hitherto claimed the attention of the world, it is probable that generations to come will see the military events as significant chiefly in that they were the prelude to the political changes, to the Russian Revolution."

zelos was unable to persuade Greece to send an army because the King opposed the project. Had this army been sent in February the Gallipoli Peninsula would have been taken, because it was unfortified, and Greece would have admitted the Allies to Constantinople. But the King vetoed the proposal and the veto received the endorsement of a people who accepted the decision of the soldier Constantine over the advice of the civilian Venizelos. The King said that the operation was a military impossibility. ·To the Greek the judgment of the victor of Kilkis stood irrefutable.

Once more, when the Allies sent their armies to the peninsula, Venizelos sought to send Greek contingents, as Sardinia had sent troops to the Crimea. But again the King interfered, dissolved the Boulé, forced an election, and in the period before the election the Allied operations had taken such a turn that even Venizelos could no longer confute the military judgment of the Greek sovereign. The Dardanelles campaign was failing as Constantine had forecast.

Unhappily for Venizelos, his worst obstacle was Allied diplomacy. To placate Bulgaria the cession of Kavala was demanded of Greece. To this Venizelos was willing to consent, did consent, accepting in return the promise of Smyrna and the Greek shore of Asia Minor. But the King promptly interposed his veto. He had conquered Kavala once, after Venizelos had signed it away; should it be resigned again after so much sacrifice? Delegations of the Greek populations of the whole Trans-Struma region filled Athens. They gave force to the words of the King. Greece stood with its sovereign against its statesman.

The entrance of Italy brought a new complication. Italy had taken Rhodes and the Dodecaneses in her Libyan War. These islands were as Greek as Athens itself. Italy had vetoed the union of northern Epirus with Greece after the First Balkan War and reserved these districts, also Hellenic by tongue and tradition, for herself, temporarily including them in the patchwork state of Albania, which had now crumbled to ruin. Greek troops were again in northern Epirus, but Rome had insisted that the occupation should be recognized as temporary.

Italy was the one rival of the Greeks in the eastern Mediterranean. Italy sought to rebuild the Venetian Empire of the Ægean and to lay hold upon the cities and provinces of Asia Minor and the islands of the Ægean, which had been Hellenic in their population and their tradition since the remote days when they had provoked a Persian invasion by a resistance to another great and predatory empire. When Italy entered the war Greek sympathy with the Allies naturally and visibly cooled. When the Allies promised the Greeks Smyrna after the war against the cession of Kavala without delay, the Greek public rallied to the side of the King who opposed the cession.

For months this sordid comedy went on. Ferdinand demanded for Bulgaria, as the price of adherence to the Allies, provinces which the Serb hesitated to yield, the Rumanian refused to cede, or the King of Greece roused his subjects to patriotic fury by declining to surrender.

In all this it is impossible not to believe that Ferdinand and Constantine played together, because, when the Germans did come south, Constantine not only abandoned the Kavala district to the Bulgars, but directed the Greek garrison to surrender the forts, the garrisons, and the guns to the invader. Inevitably one is bound to conclude that the mission of Ferdinand and Constantine was to engage the Allies in impossible negotiations until the right moment arrived and then to throw off the mask. And never was a game more skillfully played.

In all this time Allied diplomacy wholly failed to see the truth. It still dreamed of restoring the Balkan League which Sir Edward Grey had allowed to be slain at the Conference of London. While Germany promised Bulgaria and Greece territory not theirs as the reward of service, the Allies besought Greece and Serbia to surrender what they possessed to a Bulgaria known both by the Serbs and the Greeks to be actually bound by promises to the Central Powers and ready at any moment to transform the promises into performances.

And while Allied diplomacy was asking the Balkan States to make sacrifices for its friendship, Allied prospects and prestige were rapidly falling. Bulgar and Greek soldiers alike had fought and conquered the Turk. The victors of Lule Burges and Yenidze-Vardar looked with amazement upon the failure of French and British troops at Gallipoli, where they confronted armies which had been driven out of Europe, save for Constantinople and Gallipoli, in the few weeks of the opening act of the First Balkan War. In the same fashion Russian disasters in Galicia and Poland made new echoes in Sofia and Athens.

Had the Allies in May, 1915, sent to Salonica some of the troops which they wasted on the Gallipoli Peninsula, Greece would have been stampeded into the war and even Bulgaria might have broken away from its king. Backed by Allied men and fleets Venizelos could have carried Greece with him. At the least Serbia would have been saved and Bulgaria would have remained neutral. And Serbia, the faithful soldier of the Allies, was the only certain element in the situation. Yet to the end Allied diplomacy sought, not to save Serbia, but to compel the Serbs to make sacrifices; and those sacrifices, at last agreed to by Belgrade, were announced almost at the moment when Bulgaria was ready to strike.

### V. THE FINAL FOLLY

But the supreme miscalculation of the Allies was in their estimate of the contemporary value in the Balkans of a treaty made in different circumstances to cover wholly dissimilar conditions. After the Second Balkan War the victors, Rumania, Serbia, and Greece, had framed an alliance not unlike that made by the three states which had partitioned Poland. In case of a Bulgarian attack upon any one of the contracting nations, the other two were bound to make the attack a *casus belli*.

Hence London and Paris at all times remained confident that, if Bulgaria should enter the war and attack Serbia, Rumania and Greece, faithful to their agreement, would spring to the aid of the Serb. To the very end Sir Edward Grey, and presumably Delcassé, clung to this belief. Yet no belief could have been more unwarranted. Germany had torn up her treaty guaranteeing the neutrality of Belgium. She had done this merely because she needed an avenue of approach to an enemy she sought to strike down. Would Rumania and Greece hesitate to ignore another "scrap of paper" when their existence would be imperilled by fulfilling their commitments?

Bulgaria having definitely committed herself to the Central Powers by the agreement of July 17, began to mobilize within a brief time. Turkey solemnly ceded to her old foe the strip of territory west of the Maritza along which ran the railroad from Sofia and Philippopolis to Dedeagatch, the sole Bulgarian seaport. There was now no question as to Bulgarian purpose. But still the Allies hesitated. A despairing cry came from Belgrade. "Let us attack the Bulgar before he is mobilized," the Serb cried. But the stern moralists of London and Paris, still listening to Ferdinand's soft words, his assurances that he was mobilizing solely for defensive purposes, forbade the Serb and sealed his doom.

While Bulgaria was mobilizing, Constantine and Venizelos alike consented to Greek mobilization. But subsequently, when the mask was off, and Constantine kept Greece neutral, Bulgaria declared war upon Serbia. The situation was this: A great Russian army was, seemingly, on the point of capture about Vilna. All Russian armies were in retreat after a summer of unparalleled disaster. Russia was out of the war for months—Berlin said forever. The victor of the Dunajec was at the Danube with a strong army and a huge park of artillery. Austrian and German troops were at the Rumanian borders and Rumania was powerless.

Accordingly Rumania renounced her obligations—to do otherwise would have been to invite the ruin that came soon enough, as it turned out. There was left Greece. Should she, without Allied assistance—for no Allied troops were immediately available—undertake the task of holding off the whole Bulgar army while Serbia struggled with Mackensen? The end of that struggle was assured from the outset, for the Serbs had no heavy artillery. Granted that the Bulgars were checked for the time, what would happen when Mackensen had disposed of the Serbs, as he was bound to dispose of them in a few short weeks?

The pathway of honour was clear. But Rumania, with a considerable army and a frontier touching Russia, had renounced it. Was it likely that Greece would seek to earn the glory that Belgium had acquired by inviting the fate which Belgium had met, which Serbia was now about to meet, which Rumania faced one short year later? The Allies believed so to the end. In the closing hours Sir Edward Grey offered Greece Cyprus as compensation for fulfilling her obligations. Venizelos endeavoured to lead his country along the pathway of duty, the duty which he still saw. But with the consent of most of his subjects Constantine intervened, Venizelos fell and went out of power. Greece declared her neutrality and Serbia was left to perish.

Constantine's decision cost him his crown. It was a decision which had been reached long in advance of the fact. His bad faith was soon to become notorious. He had ruined the Allied hopes at the Dardanelles when there was still a chance of victory in February and March. He had kept Greece neutral in later months before Germany was ready to strike, when Greek participation might have been really useful to the Allies and of permanent profit to his country. But when, in September, 1915, he intervened to keep Greece out of the war, he acted in accord with the will of his countrymen. The heavy artillery of Mackensen along the Danube was already making echoes in Athens.

Looking backward it is plain to see the extent of Allied folly. In the Balkans, men, money, and guns alone count. No Balkan state has any reason to trust the Concert of Europe or the component parts thereof. Again and again what has been won by Balkan blood has been returned to the Turk by European statesmanship. From San Stefano to the Conference of London the story is the same. Experience, bitter experience, has made realists of the Balkan peoples, and it was only by recognizing this fact that the Allies could hope to draw profit out of the Near East.

Yet of the four considerable states, three—Serbia, Rumania, and Greece—were always friendly to the Allies. One entered the war in 1914, another in 1916, and the third in 1917. Had they entered at the outset or at any moment before Midsummer, 1915, this fact would have spelled disaster to the Central Powers. All could have been enlisted before the summer of 1915 and even Bulgaria might have been bought by concessions, after the Bulgars saw their neighbours enlisted. The Pro-Russian party at Sofia might have disposed of the Austrian Czarlet, none too popular after the Second Balkan War.

But unless the Allies were willing to send men and guns, armies and fleets to the Near East—troops to Serbia, fleets to Salonica—there was no chance of a favourable outcome in 1915. When the Allies sent their troops to Gallipoli they disposed of their last strategic reserve. Division after division disappeared in the mud and dust of Gallipoli. These divisions would have saved Serbia, enlisted Greece, impressed Bulgaria. But the Allied attention was focussed, not upon the Danube but upon the Dardanelles. The consequence was the Serbian tragedy, with its concomitant circumstances which changed the whole character of the war.

In July, 1914, Sir Edward Grey utterly failed to grasp the European situation. He could not face the facts. He continued to base his action upon his ideals and his aspirations. His failure was inevitable, but it was less to be condemned, perhaps, because all efforts were doomed to fail in the presence of inescapable war. In the Balkans, on the other hand, Grey had every chance. As usual his purposes were honourable, his methods above reproach; but his failure was more complete than anything in recent British history, and few failures have been more expensive in all history.

In the past, British foreign ministers have not infrequently been reproached with having displayed more perspicacity than principle. Sir Edward Grey's Balkan policy combined the maximum of principle with the irreducible minimum of perspicacity. His character and good repute survived the shock of all his defeats. But his country narrowly escaped permanent injury and his administration of British foreign policy made it the jest of the world.

The spectacle of the successor of Disraeli tricked, duped, played with, by a Bulgarian Czarlet must remain as the extreme contrast to the scene at the Congress of Berlin, where Beaconsfield divided with Bismarck the authority of Europe. The Balkan episode finally led to the fall of Grey as it promptly eliminated Delcassé. But, unhappily, opportunity in the east had preceded Sir Edward; he might return, it would not.

# CHAPTER THIRTEEN

## THE SERBIAN TRAGEDY

### I

### SERBIA'S PROBLEM

The story of the Serbian campaign is briefly told.  At the outset of the war Serbia had the best army of its size in Europe.  It had destroyed the Turkish Macedonian Army at Kumanovo in 1912, winning one of the most decisive victories in the history of war.  It had completed its achievement at Monastir in a struggle of real importance although little known to the world, and its aid to the Bulgar had made the capture of Adrianople possible.  Indeed, the Turkish commander had surrendered his sword to a Serb, not to a Bulgar.

In the Second Balkan War, the victory of Bregalnitza, won after a treacherous attack by the Bulgarians during a truce, had cleared Macedonia of Ferdinand's troops and decided the issue of the war.  At the Jedar Serbia had won the first great victory for the Allies in the World War and again at Valievo had routed and destroyed an Austrian force.  Despite the horrors of the typhus epidemic of the winter of 1914-15 the Serb armies still held the line of the Danube and the Save—that of the Dwina had no longer a military value, since two attempts by the Austrians had proven that this was not the road to Nish.

With something like 150,000 veteran troops Marshal Putnik faced the gathering hosts of Mackensen.  Behind him the railroad ran clear to Salonica through Nish, and from Salonica he drew his munitions and supplies from Allied ships.  As long as this road remained open the escape of the Serb army was assured and the Serbs could calculate that before they had been driven south of the Morava Valley, aid would come to them from the western powers.  The sole weakness of the Serb army, of real moment, was its lack of heavy guns.  Behind the great Danube and the considerable Save its trench lines were admirable.

They far surpassed those of Radko Dimitrieff at the Dunajec. Yet before such a concentration of artillery as had won the Dunajec it was always clear Serbian defence must crumble.

But if the Serb position against an attack from the north was fairly satisfactory—wholly satisfactory save in the matter of heavy artillery —the menace of a Bulgarian attack from the east was unmistakable. Coming south from Belgrade the Vienna-Salonica railroad, after it leaves Nish, the temporary capital of Serbia, approaches the Bulgarian frontier. It is not a day's march from the border at Vranja. It then turns west again, but below Uskub, in the Vardar Valley, it again draws near to the territory of Ferdinand.

Should the Bulgarians enter the war and push west, as they were bound to do, then the Serbs recognized from the outset that the Salonica railroad would shortly be cut, unless the Allies were able to send aid in time. If the railroad was ut, then the Serbs would lose their line of munitionment and their single avenue of escape to their Allies at Salonica. There would then be left only the mountain tracks from Prisrend down the Drin Valley to Scutari and Durazzo, or up the Black Drin Valley to Ochrida and Monastir. And a Bulgar advance to Monastir would cut this road.

The Balkan winter was in sight and retreat through these regions —utterly lacking in roads, in food supply, inhabited by hostile Albanian tribes—meant the probable destruction of the Serb army under conditions more terrible than those which overwhelmed the Grand Army on its retreat from Moscow. As long as the peril came only from the north the Serb could make head. He could oppose a gallant resistance and by a slow retreat make his way down to the Ægean, where he would find supplies and supports. His fate depended upon the Allied ability to cover his retreat between Nish and Salonica against the Bulgarian attack.

As early as September 19 the first shells of Mackensen fell in Belgrade and the same day Nish reported that Bulgaria was mobilizing. On September 27 came the despairing appeal of the Serbs to be permitted to attack Bulgaria, still mobilizing. But Ferdinand told the Allies and

the Allies told the Serbs that there was nothing to be feared from this
mobilization; and since Greece, too, was mobilizing, London and Paris
were satisfied that a Greek army would be ready to cover the Serb
communications if Bulgaria entered the war.

But on October 11 Bulgarian troops at last crossed the Serbian
frontier.  Venizelos fell, Constantine proclaimed his neutrality, and
Serbia's sole hope now lay in the ability of the Allies to get troops from
Gallipoli to the Vardar before the small Serb force in this region was
disposed of.

## II.  GERMAN AND BULGAR

We have now to examine a twofold operation.  Mackensen, with
two armies, crossed the Danube between October 7 and 11, east and
west of Belgrade.  Thereafter his troops pushed south slowly, their
heavy artillery preparing the way.  His objective was Nish, where he
aimed to make junction with the Bulgars, who were coming west out of
Sofia and by Pirot.

The Bulgars, in the meantime, were pushing three forces west.
They moved along one side of the Serbia square, the eastern, as the
Germans moved along the northern.  One Bulgar army moved up the
Danube to join hands with the Germans who had crossed the river
east of Belgrade.  When they met the Danube would be cleared
and one line of communication between Bulgaria and her Allies—between Berlin and Constantinople—would be open.  A second Bulgarian army advanced toward Nish, seeking to cut off the Serbs to the
north from their capital and also to cut the Belgrade-Salonica railroad.  Finally a third Bulgarian army, the most important, pushed
over the low passes from Kustendil and moved at the Salonica railroad in the Varda Valley with Veles as their first and Uskub as their
ultimate objective.  October 17 saw the Nish-Salonica line cut near
Vranja.

Meantime, on October 5, the first Allied troops had landed at
Salonica, disregarding the formal protest of the Greek government.
By October 12 Sarrail had arrived and taken command and while
the British pushed a division out toward the Struma to cover the flank,

the French moved up the Vardar Valley and by October 19 were at
Strumnitza station, just across the Serb frontier.   Eight days later
they were at Kriviolak.   Here was the desperate crisis of the campaign.

On October 20, while the French were just passing Strumnitza,

THE DESTRUCTION OF SERBIA

The black area denotes the territory of the Central Powers.
The checkered area shows neutral territory.
Note how Serbia was cut off from Saloniki, whence the Allied relief was to come.

a strong Bulgar army had reached Veles and thus definitely cut the
Salonica-Nish railroad.   Two days later they were at Uskub; a wedge
was thus inserted between the Serbs and their Allies.   Unless the wedge
could be removed the position of the Serb army to the north was critical.   Still, even at this moment, there was left the road south via
Prisrend, Dibra, and Ochrida to Monastir, provided that the Serbs—hold-

ing Babuna Pass, the gateway to Monastir from the Vardar valley near Veles—could hang on until Sarrail arrived. And on November 5 the French were less than ten miles from the Serbs at Babuna Pass.

Once more, however, the Allies had come too late. Babuna Pass was now forced, the Serbs flung back upon Monastir, which was indefensible, and the French troops found themselves in deadly peril in their dangerously advanced positions along the Vardar south of the Babuna. There was nothing for it but to retreat rapidly, and in the next few days the French were drawn back to the Greek frontier, while the Bulgars pushed in from Monastir.

Meantime Mackensen's armies had moved slowly. They were awaiting the moment when the Serb retreat should be cut off before seeking a decision. The time had come and German activity was now redoubled. The only roads open to the Serb armies to reach the seacoast, to escape from the far-flung net, were by the Drin through Prisrend or over the Montenegrin Mountains; and the Bulgarians pushing north from Uskub were forcing the Katchanik Gorge and threatening these remaining roads.

What followed was not war but tragedy. In the next few weeks the wreck of Putnik's army, together with thousands of Serb peasants, fled over the Albanian Mountains down to the Adriatic. Thousands and thousands perished of hunger, of cold. The army which reached the shores of the Adriatic was an army of skeletons, not soldiers. Nor was Scutari a safe halting place, for Austrian troops were pushing south through Montenegro. Still southward the remnant of the Serbs pressed, now attacked by Albanian bands in Austrian pay.

Yet the marvel of this episode is not the number of Serbians that perished, but the number that escaped. Thanks to the Italian navy many thousands actually got away to Corfu and there on that island was presently assembled the Serbian government, the Serbian army, all that was left of independent Serbia. The fate of Belgium had now overtaken another little people and King Peter, like King Albert, had waited in vain for his allies. The loss of Belgium was inevitable, but the Serbian tragedy was the more terrible because it was unnecessary.

III.   THE END OF THE EASTERN CAMPAIGN

On November 28 the German Government announced the end of the campaign in the Balkans.   The remnant of the Serb army had fled into the mountains of Albania.   All of Serbia and Montenegro were either in Bulgarian and German hands or soon would be.   More than 100,000 prisoners had been captured and most of the Serb field artillery and equipment.   Forty thousand square miles had been occupied besides northern Albania, which was destined to fall to Austrian and Bulgar forces at no distant date.

As for the Anglo-French forces, they were back in Greece, covering Salonica.   Their position was not unlike that of Wellington in the lines of Torres Vedras, but with the difference that the Kaiser could leave to his peninsular allies the task of containing this army whereas Napoleon could not assign a similar task to the Spanish.

But the essential fact was that the Germans had now broken down the Serbian barrier between their Turkish ally and themselves.   The Danube and the Bulgarian railroads provided an immediate road for men and munitions sent from Germany to Gallipoli.   The Belgrade-Sofia-Constantinople railroad, temporarily wrecked by the Serbs, would soon be restored.   The British position on Gallipoli had long been recognized as hopeless, so far as offensive success was concerned, but it had now become perilous by reason of the arrival of German troops and guns at the Golden Horn.   It was no longer a question of taking Constantinople, but of saving the Allied army.

More than this the Salonica problem became daily more pressing. The folly of divergent operations, "side shows," was now apparent and there was an insistent demand to abandon Salonica, since Serbia was lost. But this meant to abandon Serbia permanently and to give Greece over to the Germans, for no one could doubt that the moment the Allies left Salonica, Constantine would welcome his brother-in-law to Athens and Greece would follow Bulgaria into the orbit of the Central Powers.

After long delays the Allies decided to stay—the voice of France was emphatic, although Joffre objected and Kitchener protested.   To abandon Serbia was to kill all chance of Rumanian aid. It was to surrender the Balkans to the Germans. It was also to insure an attack at Suez. But if the decision to stay was sound, it carried with it very obvious disadvantages, not the least of which was that of imposing a real burden upon transport to supply a huge army overseas. It locked up troops which would be needed on the western front. It consumed men and munitions on a minor operation and against Bulgaria, not Germany.

The evacuation of Gallipoli was now assured and the transfer of some of the troops to Salonica would reduce the burden of the Allies in the east, but Britain was at this very moment pushing forward another "side show" far off in Mesopotamia, also doomed to disaster as a result of Germany's successful thrust to the Golden Horn, because at no distant date German officers were to aid Turkish troops in the capture of a British army on the Tigris. Kut-el-Amara in the next spring is a very real consequence of the German success in the Balkans in the autumn of 1915.

The Serbian tragedy is not the last act in the Balkan drama. Another year was to see Rumania destroyed, this time by treachery not folly—by Russian betrayal, not by British or French fatuity. But with the fall of Serbia the Balkans were lost to the Allies. The main purpose of Germany before the war was now achieved in one campaign. The great barrier between Turkey and Germany, erected by the two Balkan Wars to the great satisfaction of Britain, France, and Russia, was in ruins. Austria, backed by Germany, had risked a World War rather than permit this Serbian barrier to endure. It had fallen now; it had fallen at the hour when Russia also lay in ruins; it had fallen in one of the most brilliant campaigns of the war, inexpensive as it was short. And the campaign had not committed Germany to new expenditures of men. On the contrary, it had provided Bulgar and Osmanli divisions to serve German ends and released Austrian armies for service against Italy.

In all respects, the Balkan campaign was for the Kaiser a fortunate episode in a fortunate year. It made a happy last act to a drama which quite justly filled Germany with confidence as to the future and complete satisfaction as to the past.

# CHAPTER FOURTEEN

## THE END OF THE CAMPAIGN

### I

### THE ACHIEVEMENT

The campaign of 1915 ends with the Balkan operations. Between the campaigns of 1914 and 1915 there is no clear frontier. If in the west the termination of the First Battle of Ypres supplies a dividing line in late November, the operations in the east continued without cessation all through the winter. Austria's peril compelled untiring and incessant German effort. But between the campaigns of 1915 and 1916 there is a distinct break and the end of that campaign which we have now examined is one of the memorable moments of the first three years of the war.

At the close of 1914 the Germans were faced with the fact that on the larger side they had failed. The Marne and its succeeding phases from the Aisne to the Yser had been a defeat, their major purposes had not been realized, and while this was the situation in the west, in the east Austria was unmistakably beaten and threatened with complete collapse. The real as contrasted with the apparent situation at the end of the year 1914 was unfavourable to the Germans.

A year later the change had been almost immeasurable. German armies had marched from victory to victory. More than a hundred thousand square miles of Russian territory, with a population of twenty odd millions, had been occupied. Poland, Courland, Volhynia, were in German hands. Only Riga, of all the towns marked by the Pan-Germans on the eastern marches of Teutonism, had escaped Hindenburg and Mackensen, and Riga was always to be had for a price—was, in fact, to fall ultimately without the payment of any price. Warsaw, Libau, Vilna, Grodno, Kovno, Brest, Bielostok, Lomza, Lublin, Ivangorod—who could count the number or tell the names of all the cities taken?

And in addition, thirty thousand square miles of Austrian territory had been rescued. On New Year's Day, 1915, Russian troops were occupying most of Galicia and the Bukovina; they even clung to a material fragment of East Prussia itself. Now all was changed. Only a few thousand square miles—a thin strip about Tarnopol—remained of Russian conquests. And Russia herself was beaten, was doomed to fall the prey, first to as tate of reaction and then of revolution. Time would complete the work begun by Mackensen at the Dunajec, even though Brusiloff was to win a few great battles in Galicia before the ultimate crash came.

Turning southward Germany had broken through the wall that separated her from Turkey. Serbia had fallen and more than forty thousand square miles of Balkan territory were at Germany's command and in the hands of her allies. Bulgaria had enlisted and the Bulgar army was a new weapon in the armoury of the German General Staff. Turkish man-power was now at the service of German drill sergeants. Constantine was but waiting for a German army of deliverance to throw his country into the hands of the master of Central Europe.

In the west the German line had held; the conquests of August and September, 1914, were still intact: the mineral districts of France, of Belgium; the factories of the Latin north. From Antwerp to the Golden Horn, from Scutari to the Gulf of Alexandretta, German railroads bore men and munitions; down the Hedjaz railway from Aleppo were moving the advance guards of the force that was to assail Egypt through Suez when the right moment came. The British army at Gallipoli was condemned to evacuation and might be captured. The Allied force at Salonica was impotent for a long period. The British army in Mesopotamia had already involved itself in ruin and was presently to surrender.

In sum, the eastern situation had been disposed of, while the western perils had been arrested. Germany had eliminated Russia, as she had sought to eliminate France in the campaign of 1914. She was now free to try again. England was unready—could not be ready for six months. Russia was incapable of any effort in this same period. The Balkan situation was satisfactory and would remain so for two years,

finally changing only to a still more favourable aspect with the destruction of Rumania and the onset of the Russian Revolution.

There was left only France, stricken but resolute, mutilated but
still opposing strong armies and an unshaken spirit. Between Germany

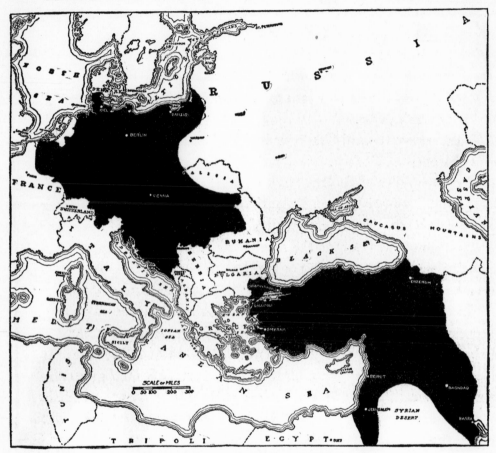

THE GROWTH OF MIDDLE EUROPE—A
The territory occupied by Germany and her Allies in April, 1915

and supreme victory France was the single remaining obstacle, and
German hands were now free to deal with France, far freer than they
had been in August and September, 1914.

## II.   GERMAN SPIRIT

Despite all Allied calculations, too, the Germans were neither starving nor dejected.   The war had turned out longer than they had fore-

seen; the first attempt had not brought the complete victory expected, but it had brought results that endured upon the map; while the campaign against Russia and the march to the Golden Horn had fired the Teutonic mind and set in motion an imagination which is ever active

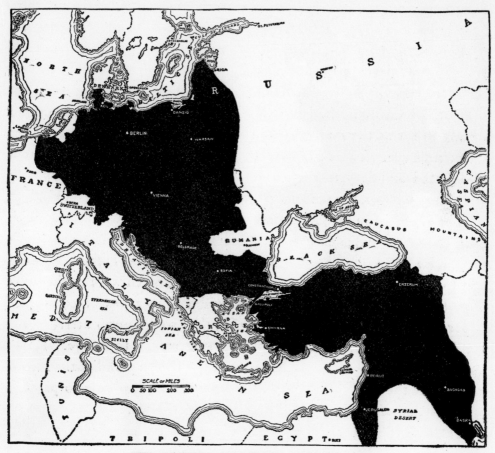

THE GROWTH OF MIDDLE EUROPE—B
Middle Europe completed: the situation on December 31, 1915

when German progress is in the picture. The British blockade had not brought actual misery. It had only begun to bring moderate privation.

The German people wanted peace, but so did all peoples; and the German people, looking with natural pride upon what had been accomplished, could believe their leaders who declared that one more great effort would bring peace, victorious peace, peace with its subsequent prosperity already insured by the German expansion from the Baltic to the Persian Gulf. Mitteleuropa was a fact. The German place in the sun desired by all Germans was stamped on every map of Europe. It remained only to have a final reckoning with a blind and obstinate France who refused to face facts that were undeniable, which appealed from the map to the imaginations of their statesmen and newspapers.

London, Paris, New York did not see the things as they were and therefore could not grasp the German emotion. They could not perceive, because the British and French press missed the facts; could not realize that Germany had won the war, won her main objectives, not merely so far as the map was concerned, but also in the minds of the German people. These newspapers continued to describe the Germans as dejected and desperate when German optimism was still mounting and German hopes, temporarily shaken in 1914, again taking on vitality.

The German, on his side, believed that the Allies saw things with his eyes, knew themselves defeated and merely uttered vain boasts and idle prophecies to cover chagrin and despair. If the French believed him to be starving, he was convinced that the French were at the point of moral and material exhaustion. For him France was "bled white." As for the British, he was convinced that they would never arrive. And the German still believed that they never meant to arrive. As he thought the Gaul unstable, so he believed the Briton perfidious. He believed that the British nation was incapable and unwilling to pay the price in blood of continental warfare on the new scale.

Through the neutral press and the neutral correspondent the two camps trumpeted forth their conflicting claims. Each saw a part of the truth hidden to the other and affirmed that the other was dealing in wilful mendacity and calculated dishonesty. This was the strangest war ever carried on, but it should have been enlightening to those whose business it was to analyze the evidence that came from opposite camps. Yet German statesmen solemnly informed their fellow countrymen that the French and British people, already knowing themselves beaten, were wickedly driven to slaughter by Briand and Grey (sic). While British and French statesmen encouraged the absurd belief that Germany was crumbling to her ruin, her armies despairing, her civilians starving.

Of the two views it is impossible not to believe that the German was more nearly in accordance with contemporary fact. All the actual gain, all the immediate profit in Europe, had been German and it had been colossal. The task was not completed, but much, very much, had been done. The German was right about the map. He was also right about his own will to conquer. His only error was in believing that his foe was both beaten and conscious of defeat. He was ignorant, too, of the terrible consequences of the crimes of his armies. He could not know that his enemies were prepared, and for long would remain prepared, to die in defeat rather than live under conditions imposed by a German victory, because of the deeds of German soldiers.

For the peoples at war with Germany the contest had become a spiritual contest. It remained for the German a material thing and on the material side his victory seemed incontestable. Actually the war was of course still undecided; the Germans had miscalculated the extent of their success; the Allies had underestimated German strength and the capacity of the German nation for organization and endurance. The first campaign had been a German defeat, the second a great German victory, but there were to be a third and a fourth, reducing to dust the calculations of each contestant, making the beliefs of each in 1915 seem ridiculous in 1917. And yet, since out of these mistaken calculations and conceptions grew the subsequent decisions and the later military operations, their value to the student of history is manifest.

### III. A WONDERFUL YEAR

Until the coming of the World War, men had been accustomed to turn to the pages which describe the Napoleonic cycle and read and re-read with unfailing wonder the narrative of those mighty campaigns of the young Emperor—Austerlitz, Jena, Friedland—which in three years made him master of Europe. At their close he had surrounded France with subject states. Italy was a dependency, the Confederation of the Rhine a tool, the Grand Duchy of Warsaw a paper creation, subject to his pleasure. The map of Europe of 1807 is the final demonstration of the magnitude of French achievement.

Yet it seems far from unlikely that when the World War has become as remote as the Napoleonic struggle seemed in the last years of the Nineteenth Century, German achievement of 1915 will have acquired something like the glamour, the marvellous character that the Napoleonic possessed for the generation that was middle-aged when the World War came.

Between May and December German armies marched into Warsaw and Vilna, Belgrade and Constantinople. German domination descended from the Danube to the Morava, from the Morava to the Vardar; it passed the Balkans and tarried briefly at the Golden Horn; it passed over into Asia and arrived at Suez and Bagdad. The victory of the Dunajec had immediate and eventual consequences beyond those of any single Napoleonic victory. What Napoleon failed to do in the Iberian Peninsula, the Kaiser achieved in the Balkan.

Russia, France, Britain, Italy, Belgium, Serbia were allied against the German with all their great resources and all the great resources of their colonies. The United States became in fact, if not admittedly, the workshop and the granary of the Allies. Yet in the face of the most tremendous coalition known to history, the German in 1915 marched from victory to victory. Though another Leipzig and another Waterloo abolish this empire and the material consequences of this achievement, is it too much to believe that it will endure in legend and history, even though not one evidence survives upon the map to testify to the German conquests of 1915?

New Germany, like the New France born of the Revolution, went forth to fight the world and in 1915 her fight rivalled the struggle of France on the military and material side. Between January and December, 1915, the Germans built an empire comparable only to the creation of Napoleon. They remade the map of Europe and stretched a mailed hand across the Hellespont to Asia Minor. Dreams and aspirations at which Europe had laughed for a quarter of a century became realities.

To the nations and peoples she conquered, Germany did not, like

France a century before, carry any new gospel. Her coming did not free serfs or spread the ideal of personal liberty. Her faith was the sterile faith of force. To those who yielded she brought order of the uncompromising sort; to those who resisted she brought death. Her pathway was indicated by ruin, and peoples as well as rulers fled before her armies. Her progress was marked by slaughter and by ashes. Hers was a conquest like to that of the successors of Mohammed. One idea and one alone possessed her soldiers and her statesmen—she condemned those whom she conquered to become Teutonic or perish; she spared neither the monuments of the past, which came within range of her artillery, nor the women of her enemies whose destruction or dishonour might serve a German end. Wherever her armies passed they sowed hatred and aroused resentment. But in their power, in their force, there was something that inspired awe as does the thunderbolt.

And in 1915 the German might was still unchecked. The confidence of the German people in victory, the belief of the German race in its high destiny and world mission, was unshaken. From Ostend to the environs of Riga, from the Elbe to the Euphrates, German will was absolute, German power unchallenged. One of the mightiest empires of history had been erected and there remained only the task of making its foundations secure against another Napoleonic débâcle.

### IV. CONCLUSION

With the close of the Balkan campaign the second phase of the World War, as I see it, comes to an end. Already German guns were being assembled in the Forest of Gremilly under Verdun for the third act. In the first, Germany had sought to crush western civilization. Her failure at the Marne had been the central episode in the first phase. In the second she had assailed Russia, the east; and her success had been complete, her victory at the Dunajec one of the great victories of human history.

In this second phase Germany had erected her long-contemplated Mitteleuropa upon the ruins of Russian military power and Serbian independence. It remained to perpetuate this Mitteleuropa by a final victory in a new conflict with the west. The decision of the Marne must be reopened and Germany had already chosen her battle-ground along the Meuse. At the Dunajec, in her Russian campaign and her Balkan promenade, Germany had fashioned a new weapon, a new method of attack. On her experience at the Dunajec she had based a new system of attack which she purposed to employ against France. It was not with any vainglorious words that the Kaiser bade his soldiers endure one more campaign which should be short and bring peace. He believed what he said and his belief was warranted, although his faith was misplaced.

And as the Marne and the Dunajec were the central episodes in the first two phases of the World War, Verdun was to supply the unity for the third. At Verdun Germany was to make her second bid for world supremacy. Failing, she was to lose the offensive and stand at bay, while the superior numbers, resources, and weapons of her enemies at last began to break her lines. She was to be driven to the submarine warfare which would draw the United States into the contest at the moment Russia retired from the battle line, and transform the war from a struggle of Europe with the Teuton to a crusade of the World against the German Empire.

All this belongs to another phase, yet it must be considered in estimating the situation as the second phase closed. On January 1, 1916, Germany was at the highest point in her history, and while she prepared for the final blow—methodically, meticulously, with a clear vision as to the issues—her enemies still chattered about her imaginary ills and their even more imaginary successes. Neither the French nor the British people saw the war as it was—saw Germany as she actually existed. Not until the Kaiser's troops stood on the ruins of Fort Douaumont and approached the last line of Verdun's defences was the truth to be realized in London, to be spoken in Paris. As the second phase ended the most tremendous blow that was ever levelled against a nation was preparing, and one will search in vain through all the Allied press to detect a contemporary appreciation of the real situation.

There is a legend of Napoleon at St. Helena, which describes the great Emperor, after having reviewed all the events of the Waterloo campaign, as breaking forth with the impatient exclamation: "And still I should have won." Looking at the situation as it existed in February, 1916, will there be less reason for the German in the future to make the same observation?

**THE END**

Mr. Simonds's History of the Progress
of the War Will Be Carried Forward in the Succeeding Volumes

Editor

**Date Due**

|  |  |  |  |
|--|--|--|--|
|  |  |  |  |
|  |  |  |  |
|  |  |  |  |
|  |  |  |  |
|  |  |  |  |
|  |  |  |  |
|  |  |  |  |
|  |  |  |  |
|  |  |  |  |
|  |  |  |  |
|  |  |  |  |